crocheted cats

T0408102

crocheted cats

**FABULOUS FELINE PATTERNS
FOR PILLOWS, ACCESSORIES,
HOME DÉCOR, AND MORE**

BARBARA DONOVAN OF JOSEPH BEAR DESIGNS

CICO BOOKS

*I would like to dedicate this title to my agent Susan Mears
who has made this book possible for me.*

Published in 2025 by CICO Books
an imprint of Ryland Peters & Small Ltd
1452 Davis Bugg Road, Warrenton, NC 27589
www.rylandpeters.com

10 9 8 7 6 5 4 3 2 1

Text © Barbara Donovan 2025
Design, illustration, and photography © CICO Books 2025

The designs in this book are copyright and must not be crocheted for sale.

The author's moral rights have been asserted. All rights reserved. No part of this publication may be reproduced, stored in a retrieval system, or transmitted in any form or by any means, electronic, mechanical, photocopying, or otherwise, without the prior permission of the publisher.

US Library of Congress CIP data has been applied for.

ISBN: 978 1 80065 472 3

Printed in China

Editor: Marie Clayton
Pattern checker: Jemima Bicknell
Designer: Alison Fenton
Photographer: James Gardiner
Stylist: Nel Haynes
Illustrator: Stephen Dew

In-house editor: Jenny Dye
Art director: Sally Powell
Creative director: Leslie Harrington
Head of production: Patricia Harrington
Publishing manager: Carmel Edmonds

Note: if you are making a project for a young child or if it will be within reach of a young child, substitute the whiskers, safety nose and eyes, and any embellishments or beads with embroidery in yarn (see pages 141–142).

FSC
www.fsc.org
MIX
Paper | Supporting
responsible forestry
FSC® C008047

contents

introduction

Welcome to my second pattern book, this time a collection of crocheted cat projects. I began crocheting many years ago and soon found a love of designing and replicating animal faces. When I was asked to design a book of cat patterns I thought it would be a little challenging to offer 35 different projects. However, after a lot of research, I soon realized how wrong I was and started designing cats of all breeds and sizes, including not only domestic cats but also large wild cats. You'll find everything from a classic black-and-white cat purse to a fluffy pillow resembling the much-loved Ragdoll breed, as well as a cuddly lion toy and a cheetah pillow.

My designs are aimed at all levels of crochet so they're perfect for beginners through to more advanced crocheters. You can even recreate your own or a loved one's pet just by changing the yarn colors to produce their exact likeness. What great gifts to make for friends and family!

In this book you will find an assortment of patterns including pillows and purses, gifts for the home, and cuddly toys to suit all ages. Many of the projects can be adapted to create different designs. For example, you can easily make a pillow into a bag by omitting the pillow form, leaving the top open when you sew the front and back pieces together, and adding plastic, bamboo, or crocheted handles (see page 80). Alternatively, make a bag into a pillow by leaving out the handles and inserting a pillow form or toy fiberfill. You could even make a pillow or a bag into a pajama case to add personality to any bedroom—simply omit the handles or pillow form, and sew the front and back pieces together, leaving the top open.

The beauty of these projects is that gauge is not important. I am a very loose crocheter myself and I also know many people who are very tight with their crochet work. Whatever your gauge, you will create a cute and cuddly design.

I hope that you enjoy crocheting these designs as much as I have enjoyed designing them.

BEFORE YOU BEGIN

If you are new to crochet, turn to the Techniques section on pages 132–142 and the Abbreviations on page 142. Each project has a skill rating, from Easy (one circle) to Intermediate (two circles) and Advanced (three circles). Start with the Easy patterns then move on to the next two levels once you know the basic techniques.

CHAPTER 1
pillows

Pet cats have charmed their owners for many, many years, so what better than to have a soft cuddly pillow to remind you of your lovable pet? This pillow is worked in single and double crochet stitches with super bulky yarn which is brushed to create the soft and fluffy look for the fur.

gray cat pillow

SKILL RATING ● ● ○

YARN AND MATERIALS
King Cole Big Value Super Chunky (100% acrylic), super bulky (super chunky) weight yarn, 90yd (81m) per 3½oz (100g) ball
  4 balls of shade 024 Gray (A)
  Small amount of shade 008 Black (C)
  Length of shade 030 Pink (D)
  ¾oz (20g) shade 1758 White (E)

King Cole Truffle (100% polyamide), light worsted (DK) weight yarn, 183yd (168m) per 3½oz (100g) ball
  ⅞oz (25g) of shade 4365 Coconut (B)

Pair of 24mm safety eyes

Small amount of toy fiberfill

14in (35.5cm) round pillow form

HOOK AND EQUIPMENT
US H-8 (5mm) and US J-10 (6mm) crochet hooks

Yarn needle

Stiff brush or pet brush

Hairspray (optional)

FINISHED SIZE
Approx. 15in (38cm) diameter

ABBREVIATIONS
See page 142.

PATTERN NOTE
The Truffle yarn is worked holding two strands together in this pattern.

PILLOW FRONT AND BACK

(make 2)
Round 1: Using US J-10 (6mm) and A, ch5, join with a sl st to form a ring.
Round 2: Ch3 (counts as first dc), 11dc in ring, join with a sl st. (*12 sts*)
Round 3: Ch3, 1dc in same dc, 2dc in each dc to end, join with a sl st. (*24 sts*)
Round 4: Ch3, 2dc in next dc, [1dc in next dc, 2dc in next dc] to end, join with a sl st. (*36 sts*)
Round 5: Ch3, 1dc in next dc, 2dc in next dc, [1dc in each of next 2 dc, 2dc in next dc] to end, join with a sl st. (*48 sts*)
Round 6: Ch3, 1dc in each of next 2 dc, 2dc in next dc, [1dc in each of next 3 dc, 2dc in next dc] to end, join with a sl st. (*60 sts*)
Round 7: Ch3, 1dc in each of next 3 dc, 2dc in next dc, [1dc in each of next 4 dc, 2dc in next dc] to end, join with a sl st. (*72 sts*)
Round 8: Ch3, 1dc in each of next 4 dc, 2dc in next dc, [1dc in each of next 5 dc, 2dc in next dc] to end, join with a sl st. (*84 sts*)
Round 9: Ch3, 1dc in each of next 5 dc, 2dc in next dc, [1dc in each of next 6 dc, 2dc in next dc] to end, join with a sl st. (*96 sts*)
Round 10: Ch3, 1dc in each of next 6 dc, 2dc in next dc, [1dc in each of next 7 dc, 2dc in next dc] to end, join with a sl st. (*108 sts*)
Fasten off.

SNOUT

Round 1: Using US H-8 (5mm) hook and two strands of B held together, ch8, 1sc in 2nd ch from hook (missed ch does not count as sc), 1sc in each ch to last ch, 3sc in last ch, working along bottom of chain, 1sc in each ch to end, 1sc in end of row, join with a sl st. (*16 sts*)
Round 2: Ch1 (counts as first sc), 1sc in each of next 5 sc, [2sc in next sc] twice, 1sc in each of next 6 sc, [2sc in next sc] twice, join with a sl st. (*20 sts*)
Rounds 3–5: Ch1, 1sc in next sc, 1sc in each sc to end, join with a sl st.
Round 6: Ch1, 1sc in each of next 7 sc, [2sc in next sc] twice, 1sc in each of next 8 sc, [2sc in next sc] twice, join with a sl st. (*24 sts*)
Round 7: Ch1, 1sc in next sc, 1sc in each sc to end, join with a sl st.
Fasten off, leaving a length of yarn for forming nose.

BASE OF SNOUT

Round 1: Using US H-8 (5mm) hook and two strands of B held together, ch4, join with a sl st to form a ring.

Round 2: Ch1 (counts as first sc), 7sc in ring, join with a sl st. (*8 sts*)

Round 3: Ch1, 2sc in next sc, [1sc in next sc, 2sc in next sc] to end, join with a sl st. (*12 sts*)

Round 4: Ch1, 1sc in next sc, 1sc in each sc to end, join with a sl st.

Round 5: Ch1, 1sc in next sc, 2sc in next sc, [1sc in each of next 2 sc, 2sc in next sc] to end, join with a sl st. (*16 sts*)

Fasten off.

EARS

(make 4)

Row 1: Using US J-10 (6mm) and A, ch2.

Row 2: 1sc in 2nd ch from hook (missed ch does not count as sc). (*1 st*)

Row 3: Ch1 (counts as first sc), 1sc in same sc. (*2 sts*)

Row 4: Ch1, 1sc in same sc, 1sc in each sc to end. (*3 sts*)

Row 5: Ch1, 1sc in same sc, 1sc in each sc to end. (*4 sts*)

Row 6: Ch1, 1sc in same sc, 1sc in each sc to end. (*5 sts*)

Row 7: Ch1, 1sc in same sc, 1sc in each sc to end. (*6 sts*)

TO MAKE UP

Place front and back with right sides together. Using A, work a single crochet seam (see page 140) around, leaving an opening of approx. 6in (15cm). Turn right side out.

To form the two puffed parts of the snout, stuff the snout lightly then wind the yarn end around the center and secure firmly at the back with a stitch. Using D, embroider the mouth and nose markings. Sew the snout to the center of the pillow using the photo as a guide for positioning. Lightly stuff the base of the snout and sew in position below the snout.

Insert each safety eye into an eye surround and secure with the safety backs (see page 141). Sew eyes and surrounds above the snout using the photo as a guide for positioning.

Place two ears with wrong sides together. Using A, work a single crochet seam around all sides. Repeat with the other two ears. Sew the ears to the top of the head using the photos as a guide for positioning.

Insert the pillow form and sew the gap closed.

ADDING THE FUR

Adding the fur on the face can be done in two ways, either with a crochet hook (see page 141) or by threading each strand through with a yarn needle and then tying the ends in a knot close to the fabric. The needle is better for getting into small areas, such as around the eyes.

Face

Cut A and E into approx. 7in (18cm) lengths. Starting at the top of the snout with lengths of E, add a line of fur fringe. Add three more lines with E above the snout approx. 1in (2.5cm) apart.

Switch to A and add fur fringe around the eyes and along the sides and bottom of the snout. Continue adding lines of fur fringe with A approx. 2in (5cm) apart until you have completely covered the face. Brush and trim fur to length required so that all the fur is the same length, then trim the fur around the eyes and the first line of fur above the snout to approx. ½in (1.5cm) long.

It may be beneficial to spray the front of the pillow lightly with hairspray to keep the yarn in place (optional).

Row 8: Ch1, 1sc in same sc, 1sc in each sc to end. (7 *sts*)
Row 9: Ch1, 1sc in same sc, 1sc in each sc to end. (8 *sts*)
Row 10: Ch1, 1sc in same sc, 1sc in each sc to end. (9 *sts*)
Row 11: Ch1, 1sc in same sc, 1sc in each sc to end. (10 *sts*)
Fasten off.

EYE SURROUNDS

(make 2)
Round 1: Using US J-10 (6mm) and C, ch4, join with a sl st to form a ring.
Round 2: Ch1 (counts as first sc), 9sc in ring, join with a sl st. (10 *sts*)
Fasten off.

sunset silhouette pillow

A perfect pillow to complement the lap blanket also featured in this book (see page 38). This pattern is crocheted in the popular waffle stitch, with the cat silhouette and setting sun added to create the sunset effect.

SKILL RATING ● ● ●

YARN AND MATERIALS
King Cole Safari Chunky (100% acrylic), bulky (chunky) weight yarn, 311yd (285m) per 5¼oz (150g) ball
  2 balls of shade 5005 Sunset (A)

King Cole Moments DK (100% polyester), light worsted (DK) weight yarn, 98yd (90m) per 1¾oz (50g) ball
  2 balls of shade 474 Black (B)

King Cole Cuddles Chunky (100% polyester), bulky (chunky) weight yarn, 136yd (125m) per 1¾oz (50g) ball
  ¾oz (20g) of shade 3821 Sunflower (C)

16 x 16in (40 x 40cm) pillow form

HOOK AND EQUIPMENT
US H-8 (5mm) crochet hook
Stitch marker
Yarn needle

FINISHED SIZE
Approx. 18 x 18in (43 x 43cm)

ABBREVIATIONS
See page 142.

SPECIAL ABBREVIATION
FPdc (front post double crochet): a double crochet worked by inserting your hook around the post of the next stitch from front to back to front, rather than into the top two loops of a stitch as you normally would

PATTERN NOTE
The Moments DK yarn for the cat is worked with two strands of yarn held together throughout. It is advisable to use a stitch marker with this yarn.

PILLOW FRONT AND BACK

(make 2)

Row 1: Using A, ch52.

Row 2: 1dc in 3rd ch from hook (missed 2 ch do not count as dc), 1dc in each ch to end. (*50 sts*)

Row 3 (RS): Ch3 (counts as first dc), 1dc in next st, [1FPdc in next st, 1dc in each of next 2 sts] to end.

Row 4 (WS): Ch3, 1FPdc in next st, 1dc in next st, [1FPdc in each of next 2 sts, 1dc in next st] to last 2 sts, 1FPdc in next st, 1dc in last st.

Rep Rows 3 and 4 a further 14 times, then rep Row 3 once.

Fasten off front piece. When working back piece, do not fasten off.

Place front and back with wrong sides together. Using A, work a single crochet seam (see page 140) along three sides, working through both pieces to join; along row ends work approx. 3 sts evenly across every 2 rows. Insert pillow form then continue along fourth side to end, join with a sl st.

Edging

Round 1: Ch1 (counts as first sc), miss next 2 sc, 7dc in next sc, miss next 2 sc, [1sc in next sc, miss next 2 sc, 7dc in next sc, miss next 2 sc] to end, covering all four sides of pillow, join with a sl st.
Fasten off.

CAT FACE

Round 1: Using two strands of B held together, ch4, join with a sl st to form a ring.

Round 2: Ch1 (counts as first sc), 7sc in ring, join with a sl st. (*8 sts*)

Round 3: Ch1, 1sc in same sc, 2sc in each sc to end, join with a sl st. (*16 sts*)

Round 4: Ch1, 2sc in next sc, [1sc in next sc, 2sc in next sc] to end, join with a sl st. (*24 sts*)

Round 5: Ch1, 1sc in next sc, 2sc in next sc, [1sc in each of next 2 sc, 2sc in next sc] to end, join with a sl st. (*32 sts*)
Fasten off.

CAT EARS

(make 2)

Row 1: Using two strands of B held together, ch2.

Row 2: 1sc in 2nd ch from hook (missed ch does not count as sc). (*1 st*)

Row 3: Ch1 (counts as first sc), 1sc in same st. (*2 sts*)

Row 4: Ch1, 1sc in same st, 1sc in each sc to end. (*3 sts*)

Row 5: Ch1, 1sc in same st, 1sc in each sc to end. (*4 sts*)

Row 6: Ch1, 1sc in next sc, 1sc in each sc to end.
Fasten off.

BODY

Row 1: Using two strands of B held together, ch7.
Row 2: 1sc in 2nd ch from hook (missed ch does not count as sc), 1sc in each ch to end. (*6 sts*)
Row 3: Ch1 (counts as first sc), 1sc in same sc, 1sc in each sc to end. (*7 sts*)
Row 4: Ch1, 1sc in same sc, 1sc in each sc to end. (*8 sts*)
Row 5: Ch1, 1sc in same sc, 1sc in each sc to end. (*9 sts*)
Row 6: Ch1, 1sc in same sc, 1sc in each sc to end. (*10 sts*)
Row 7: Ch1, 1sc in same sc, 1sc in each sc to end. (*11 sts*)
Row 8: Ch1, 1sc in same sc, 1sc in each sc to end. (*12 sts*)
Rows 9–15: Ch1, 1sc in next sc, 1sc in each sc to end.
Fasten off.

TAIL

Row 1: Using two strands of B held together, ch3.
Row 2: 1sc in 2nd ch from hook (missed ch does not count as sc), 1sc in each ch to end. (*2 sts*)
Row 3: Ch1 (counts as first sc), 1sc in next sc, 1sc in each sc to end.
Rep Row 3 until work measures 3in (7.5cm).
Fasten off.

SETTING SUN

Round 1: Using C, ch4, join with a sl st to form a ring.
Round 2: Ch1 (counts as first sc), 7sc in ring, join with a sl st to first sc. (*8 sts*)
Round 3: Ch1, 1sc in same sc, 2sc in each sc to end, join with a sl st. (*16 sts*)
Round 4: Ch1, 2sc in next sc, [1sc in next sc, 2sc in next sc] to end, join with a sl st. (*24 sts*)
Round 5: Ch1, 1sc in next sc, 2sc in next sc, [1sc in each of next 2 sc, 2sc in next sc] to end, join with a sl st. (*32 sts*)
Round 6: Ch1, 1sc in each of next 2 sc, 2sc in next sc, [1sc in each of next 3 sc, 2sc in next sc] to end, join with a sl st. (*40 sts*)
Fasten off.

TO MAKE UP

Sew the cat ears to the head using the photo as a guide for positioning, then sew the head to the body. Sew the tail to body.

Pin the cat onto the pillow in the bottom left-hand corner and sew in position. Sew the setting sun onto the pillow at top right.

Sew in any yarn ends (see page 139).

YARN AND MATERIALS
King Cole Big Value Super Chunky (100% acrylic), super bulky (super chunky) weight yarn, 90yd (81m) per 3½oz (100g) ball
   4 balls of shade 3400 Brass (A)

King Cole Yummy (100% polyester), bulky (chunky) weight yarn, 131yd (120m) per 3½oz (100g) ball
   ¾oz (20g) of shade 3477 Champagne (B)

Small amount of bulky (chunky) weight yarn in black (C)

Pair of 24mm safety eyes

20mm safety nose

Toy fiberfill

14in (35.5cm) round pillow form

HOOK AND EQUIPMENT
US H-8 (5mm) and US J-10 (6mm) crochet hooks

Yarn needle

Stiff brush or pet brush

Hairspray (optional)

FINISHED SIZE
Approx. 15in (38cm) diameter

ABBREVIATIONS
See page 142.

PATTERN NOTES
As an alternative you could clip off the post from the safety nose and glue it into place. The Yummy yarn can fray very easily at either end. It is recommended that the fluff is pulled away from the cotton for the first 2in (5cm). This produces a short length of the cotton that can be sewn into the work to secure into place. To fasten off in this yarn the same procedure is used.

The faithful ginger cat is always a very popular family companion, with its pretty face and big loving eyes. This pillow is worked in simple double and single crochet stitches, making it a perfect gift for any cat lover.

ginger cat pillow

PILLOW FRONT AND BACK
(make 2)
Round 1: Using US J-10 (6mm) hook and A, ch5, join with a sl st to form a ring.
Round 2: Ch3 (counts as first dc), 11dc in ring, join with a sl st. (*12 sts*)
Round 3: Ch3, 1dc in same dc, 2dc in each dc to end, join with a sl st. (*24 sts*)
Round 4: Ch3, 2dc in next dc, [1dc in next dc, 2dc in next dc] to end, join with a sl st. (*36 sts*)
Round 5: Ch3, 1dc in next dc, 2dc in next dc, [1dc in each of next 2 dc, 2dc in next dc] to end, join with a sl st. (*48 sts*)
Round 6: Ch3, 1dc in each of next 2 dc, 2dc in next dc, [1dc in each of next 3 dc, 2dc in next dc] to end, join with a sl st. (*60 sts*)
Round 7: Ch3, 1dc in each of next 3 dc, 2dc in next dc, [1dc in each of next 4 dc, 2dc in next dc] to end, join with a sl st. (*72 sts*)
Round 8: Ch3, 1dc in each of next 4 dc, 2dc in next dc, [1dc in each of next 5 dc, 2dc in next dc] to end, join with a sl st. (*84 sts*)
Round 9: Ch3, 1dc in each of next 5 dc, 2dc in next dc, [1dc in each of next 6 dc, 2dc in next dc] to end, join with a sl st. (*96 sts*)
Round 10: Ch3, 1dc in each of next 6 dc, 2dc in next dc, [1dc in each of next 7 dc, 2dc in next dc] to end, join with a sl st. (*108 sts*)
Fasten off.

SNOUT
Round 1: Using US H-8 (5mm) hook and B, ch8, 1sc in 2nd ch from hook (missed ch does not count as sc), 1sc in each ch to last ch, 3sc in last ch, working along bottom of chain, 1sc in each ch to end, 1 sc in end of row, join with a sl st. (*16 sts*)
Round 2: Ch1 (counts as first sc), 1sc in each of next 5 sc, [2sc in next sc] twice, 1sc in each of the next 6 sc, [2sc in next sc] twice, join with a sl st. (*20 sts*)
Rounds 3–5: Ch1, 1sc in next sc, 1sc in each sc to end, join with a sl st.
Round 6: Ch1, 1sc in each of next 7 sc, [2sc in next sc] twice, 1sc in each of next 8 sc, [2sc in next sc] twice, join with a sl st. (*24 sts*)
Round 7: Ch1, 1sc in next sc, 1sc in each sc to end, join with a sl st. Fasten off, leaving a length of yarn for forming nose.

BASE OF SNOUT

Row 1: Using US H-8 (5mm) hook and B, ch4.
Row 2: 1sc in 2nd ch from hook (missed ch does not count as sc), 1sc in each ch to end. (*3 sts*)
Row 3: Ch1 (counts as first sc), 1sc in same sc, 1sc in each sc to end. (*4 sts*)
Row 4: Ch1, 1sc in same sc, 1sc in each sc to end. (*5 sts*)
Row 5: Ch1, 1sc in same sc, 1sc in each sc to end. (*6 sts*)
Fasten off.

EARS

(make 4)
Row 1: Using US J-10 (6mm) hook and A, ch2.
Row 2: 1sc in 2nd ch from hook (missed ch does not count as sc). (*1 st*)
Row 3: Ch1 (counts as first sc), 1sc in same sc. (*2 sts*)
Row 4: Ch1, 1sc in same sc, 1sc in each sc to end. (*3 sts*)
Row 5: Ch1, 1sc in same sc, 1sc in each sc to end. (*4 sts*)

Row 6: Ch1, 1sc in same sc, 1sc in each sc to end. (*5 sts*)
Row 7: Ch1, 1sc in same sc, 1sc in each sc to end. (*6 sts*)
Row 8: Ch1, 1sc in same sc, 1sc in each sc to end. (*7 sts*)
Row 9: Ch1, 1sc in same sc, 1sc in each sc to end. (*8 sts*)
Row 10: Ch1, 1sc in same sc, 1sc in each sc to end.
(*9 sts*)
Row 11: Ch1, 1sc in same sc, 1sc in each sc to end.
(*10 sts*)
Fasten off.

TO MAKE UP

Place front and back with right sides together. Using A, work a single crochet seam (see page 140) around, leaving an opening of approx. 6in (15cm). Turn right side out.

Stuff the snout and then wind the yarn end tightly around the center to form two puffed parts. Secure firmly at the back with a stitch. Using C in a yarn needle, sew the mouth markings. Push the post of the safety nose through the crochet above the mouth marking and secure with the back. Sew the snout to the center of the pillow using the photo as a guide for positioning. Stuff the base of the snout lightly then sew below the snout. Add the safety eyes above the snout and secure with the safety backs (see page 141).

Place two ears with wrong sides together. Using A, work a single crochet seam around all sides. Repeat with the other two ears. Sew the ears to the top of the head using the photos as a guide for positioning.

Insert the pillow form and sew the gap closed.

ADDING THE FUR

Adding the fur on the face can be done in two ways, either with a crochet hook (see page 141) or by threading each strand through with a yarn needle and then tying the ends in a knot close to the fabric. The needle is better for getting into small areas, such as around the eyes.

Face

Cut A into approx. 7in (18cm) lengths. Starting at the snout, add a line of fur fringing all around the snout. Add another line all around the face approx. 2in (5cm) away. Repeat until the entire pillow is covered, working a few fringes in C. Brush the yarn with a stiff brush to create the soft fur effect. Trim to length required.

It may be beneficial to spray the pillow front lightly with hairspray to keep the yarn in place (optional).

3D granny square cat pillow

This large crochet pillow would look splendid on any couch.
An easy project for the confident beginner, the pillow is crocheted
in the much-loved granny square design. The cat face is created
separately and added to the center of the pillow.

YARN AND MATERIALS

King Cole Big Value Super Chunky (100% acrylic), super bulky (super chunky) weight yarn, 90yd (81m) per 3½oz (100g) ball
   2 balls of shade 24 Gray (A)
   2 balls of shade 1758 White (B)

King Cole Explorer Super Chunky (80% acrylic, 20% wool), super bulky (super chunky) weight yarn, 80m (87yd) per 3½oz (100g) ball
   2 balls of shade 4303 Drake (C)

Small amount of black light worsted (DK) weight yarn (D)

Small amount of pink light worsted (DK) weight yarn (E)

18 x 18in (46 x 46cm) pillow form

22mm pink safety nose

Pair of 18mm safety eyes

Small amount of toy fiberfill

HOOK AND EQUIPMENT

US J-10 (6mm) crochet hook

Yarn needle

Pins

Stiff brush or pet brush

Hairspray (optional)

FINISHED SIZE

18 x 18in (46 x 46cm)

ABBREVIATIONS

See page 142.

PATTERN NOTE

This pillow cover is worked with 16 granny squares on each side. On the front, the four middle squares are crocheted in white as a background for the cat face. The back has 16 colored squares.

GRANNY SQUARE

(make 28)

Round 1: Using A, ch4, join with a sl st to form a ring.
Round 2: Ch3 (counts as first dc), 2dc in ring, ch1, [3dc in ring, ch1] 3 times, join with a sl st to top of first 3-ch, sl st in each st to next corner ch sp.
Round 3: Using C, ch3, (2dc, ch1, 3dc) in same ch sp, ch1, [(3dc, ch1, 3dc) in next ch sp, ch1] 3 times, join with a sl st, sl st in each st to next corner ch sp.
Round 4: Using B, ch3, (2dc, ch1, 3dc) in same ch sp, ch1, 3dc in next ch sp, ch1, [(3dc, ch1, 3dc) in next corner ch sp, ch1, 3dc in next ch sp, ch1] 3 times, join with a sl st.
Fasten off.

PLAIN GRANNY SQUARE

(make 4)

Using B only, work Rounds 1–4 as per granny square pattern above.
Fasten off.

CAT FACE

Round 1: Using A, ch4, join with a sl st to form a ring.
Round 2: Ch3 (counts as first dc), 11dc in ring, join with a sl st. (*12 sts*)
Round 3: Ch3, 1dc in same st, 2dc in each dc to end, join with a sl st. (*24 sts*)
Round 4: Ch3, 2dc in next dc, [1dc in next dc, 2dc in next dc] to end, join with a sl st. (*36 sts*)
Round 5: Ch3, 1dc in next dc, 2dc in next dc, [1dc in each of next 2 dc, 2dc in next dc] to end, join with a sl st. (*48 sts*)
Fasten off.

SNOUT

Round 1: Using A, ch6.
Round 2: 1sc in 2nd ch from hook (missed ch does not count as sc), 1sc in each ch to last ch, 3sc in last ch, working along bottom of chain, 1sc in each ch to end, 1sc in end of row, join with a sl st. (*12 sts*)

Round 3: Ch1 (counts as first sc), 1sc in each of next 3 sc, [2sc in next sc] twice, 1sc in each of next 4 sc, [2sc in next sc] twice, join with a sl st. (*16 sts*)
Rounds 4–6: Ch1, 1sc in next sc, 1sc in each sc to end, join with a sl st.
Sl st to center of snout.
Fasten off, leaving a length of yarn for forming snout.

BASE OF SNOUT
Round 1: Using B, ch4, join with a sl st to form a ring.
Round 2: Ch1 (counts as first sc), 7sc in ring, join with a sl st. (*8 sts*)
Fasten off.

EARS
(make 2)
Row 1: Using A, ch2.
Row 2: 1sc in 2nd ch from hook (missed ch does not count as sc). (*1 st*)
Row 3: Ch1 (counts as first sc), 1sc in same sc. (*2 sts*)
Row 4: Ch1, 1sc in same sc, 1sc in each sc to end. (*3 sts*)
Row 5: Ch1, 1sc in same sc, 1sc in each sc to end. (*4 sts*)
Row 6: Ch1, 1sc in same sc, 1sc in each sc to end. (*5 sts*)
Row 7: Ch1, 1sc in same sc, 1sc in each sc to end. (*6 sts*)
Fasten off.

TONGUE
Row 1: Using E, ch4.
Row 2: 1sc in 2nd ch from hook, 1sc in each ch to end. (*3 sts*)
Rows 3 and 4: Ch1, 1sc in same sc, 1sc in each sc to end.
Fasten off.

TO MAKE UP

Pillow back
Place two colored squares wrong sides together. Using A, work a single crochet seam (see page 140) in the back loops of each stitch along one edge to join. Repeat to join all the squares into pairs. Set aside six pairs for the front, then join the remaining pairs into rows of four squares. Finally join the rows to make up a four-by-four panel.

Pillow front
Place two plain squares wrong sides together. Using B, work a single crochet seam in the back loops of each stitch along one edge to join. Repeat to make a second pair, then join them in the same way to make a two-by-two panel. Using A, join a pair of patterned squares on each side of the panel. Join the remaining four pairs into two rows of four squares and add these rows to the top and bottom of the panel.

Joining the panels
Place the panels wrong sides together and pin. Using A, work a single crochet seam around three sides of the pillow cover making sure that you work into the stitches from both panels. Insert the pillow form and continue the single crochet seam along the fourth side to close.

Cat face
To form the two puffed parts of the snout, stuff the snout lightly then wind the yarn end around the center and secure firmly at the back with a stitch. Using E, embroider mouth markings onto the snout and sew the tongue right next to the mouth marking. Push the post of the safety nose through the crochet above the mouth marking and secure with the back. Sew the snout to front of the face, using the photo as a guide for positioning. Sew the base of the snout below the snout. Add the safety eyes above the snout and secure with the safety backs (see page 141). Clip off the surplus eye posts so that they sit flat. Using D, embroider whiskers in straight stitch (see page 141, optional).

Sew the ears to the top of the head, using the photos as a guide.

Adding the fur
Adding the fur on the face can be done in two ways, either with a crochet hook (see page 141) or by threading each strand through with a yarn needle and then tying the ends in a knot close to the fabric. The needle is better for getting into small areas, such as around the eyes.

Cut A into 6in (15cm) lengths. Add lines of fur fringing around and under the snout in layers. Continue all around the face and below the ears. Brush gently to give the fluffy look, then trim any excess fur to produce the shape required.

It may be beneficial to spray the cat face on the pillow front with hairspray to keep the yarn in place (optional).

Sew the face to the center of the four plain squares on the center front of the pillow.

What a head-turner this cheetah would be sitting on any chair or couch! This pillow is crocheted in single and double crochet stitches and brought to life with an array of colors. The beauty of this pattern is that the face markings can be varied as you create this stunning project.

cheetah pillow

SKILL RATING ● ● ●

YARN AND MATERIALS
King Cole Big Value Super Chunky (100% acrylic), super bulky (super chunky) weight yarn, 90yd (81m) per 3½oz (100g) ball
  3 balls of shade 3490 Latte (A)
  ½ ball of shade 12 Champagne (B)
  ½ ball of shade 3400 Brass (C)
  Small amount of shade 8 Black (D)

Pair of 26mm safety eyes

30mm safety nose

Small amount of toy fiberfill

14in (35.5cm) round pillow form

HOOK AND EQUIPMENT
US J-10 (6mm) crochet hook

Yarn needle

Stiff brush or pet brush

Hairspray (optional)

FINISHED SIZE
Approx. 16in (40.5cm) diameter

ABBREVIATIONS
See page 142.

PILLOW FRONT AND BACK
(make 2)
Round 1: Using A, ch5, join with a sl st to form a ring.
Round 2: Ch3 (counts as first dc), 11dc in ring, join with a sl st. (*12 sts*)
Round 3: Ch3, 1dc in same dc, 2dc in each dc to end, join with a sl st. (*24 sts*)
Round 4: Ch3, 2dc in next dc, [1dc in next dc, 2dc in next dc] to end, join with a sl st. (*36 sts*)
Round 5: Ch3, 1dc in next dc, 2dc in next dc, [1dc in each of next 2 dc, 2dc in next dc] to end, join with a sl st. (*48 sts*)
Round 6: Ch3, 1dc in each of next 2 dc, 2dc in next dc, [1dc in each of next 3 dc, 2dc in next dc] to end, join with a sl st. (*60 sts*)
Round 7: Ch3, 1dc in each of next 3 dc, 2dc in next dc, [1dc in each of next 4 dc, 2dc in next dc] to end, join with a sl st. (*72 sts*)
Round 8: Ch3, 1dc in each of next 4 dc, 2dc in next dc, [1dc in each of next 5 dc, 2dc in next dc] to end, join with a sl st. (*84 sts*)
Round 9: Ch3, 1dc in each of next 5 dc, 2dc in next dc, [1dc in each of next 6 dc, 2dc in next dc] to end, join with a sl st. (*96 sts*)
Round 10: Ch3, 1dc in each of next 6 dc, 2dc in next dc, [1dc in each of next 7 dc, 2dc in next dc] to end, join with a sl st. (*108 sts*)
Fasten off.

SNOUT
Round 1: Using B, ch5, join with a sl st to form a ring.
Round 2: Ch1 (counts as first sc), 9sc in ring, join with a sl st. (*10 sts*)
Round 3: Ch1, 1sc in next sc, 2sc in next sc, 1sc in each of next 4 sc, 2sc in next sc, 1sc in each of next 2 sc, join with a sl st. (*12 sts*)
Round 4: Ch1, 1sc in next sc, 2sc in next sc, [1sc in each of next 2 sc, 2sc in next sc] to end, join with a sl st. (*16 sts*)
Round 5: Ch1, 1sc in each of next 2 sc, 2sc in next sc, [1sc in each of next 3 sc, 2sc in next sc] to end, join with a sl st. (*20 sts*)

Round 6: Ch1, 1sc in next sc, 1sc in each sc to end, join with a sl st.

Round 7: Ch1, 1sc in each of next 3 sc, 2sc in next sc, [1sc in each of next 4 sc, 2sc in next sc] to end, join with a sl st. (*24 sts*)

Rounds 8 and 9: Ch1, 1sc in next sc, 1sc in each sc to end, join with a sl st.

Fasten off.

EARS

(make 4)

Row 1: Using A, ch6.

Row 2: 1sc in 2nd ch from hook (missed ch does not count as sc), 1sc in each ch to end. (*5 sts*)

Row 3: Ch1 (counts as first sc), 1sc in same sc, 1sc in each sc to end. (*6 sts*)

Row 4: Ch1, 1sc in same sc, 1sc in each sc to end. (*7 sts*)

Row 5: Ch1, 1sc in same sc, 1sc in each sc to end. (*8 sts*)
Row 6: Ch1, 1sc in same sc, 1sc in each sc to end. (*9 sts*)
Row 7: Ch1, 1sc in same sc, 1sc in each sc to end.
(*10 sts*)
Rows 8 and 9: Ch1, 1sc in next sc, 1sc in each sc to end.
Row 10: Sc2tog, 1sc in each sc to last 2 sc, sc2tog.
(*8 sts*)
Fasten off.

EYE SURROUNDS
(make 2)
Round 1: Using D, ch4, join with a sl st to form a ring.
Round 2: Ch1 (counts as first sc), 9sc in ring, join with
a sl st. (*10 sts*)
Fasten off.

TO MAKE UP
Place the back and front pieces of the pillow with
right sides together. Using A, work a single crochet
seam (see page 140) around, leaving an opening of
approx. 6in (15cm). Turn right side out.

Brush the snout to give a fluffy effect. Using D,
embroider the mouth markings and black spots onto
the snout. Add the safety nose and secure with the
back. Stuff the snout and sew to the front of the
pillow using the photo as a guide for positioning.

Insert the post of each eye into an eye surround
and secure with the safety back. Clip off any surplus
post. Sew the eyes to the pillow, using the photo
as a guide for positioning.

Place two ears with wrong sides together. Using A,
work a single crochet seam around all sides. Repeat
with the other two ears. Sew the ears to the top of
the pillow.

Insert the pillow form into the cover, then complete
the single crochet seam to close the gap.

Adding the fur
Adding the fur on the face can be done in two ways,
either with a crochet hook (see page 141) or by
threading each strand through with a yarn needle
and then tying the ends in a knot close to the fabric.
The needle is better for getting into small areas,
such as around the eyes. Follow the photos for
color placement of the fur.

Cut 7in (18cm) strands of each yarn shade. Begin
by adding two lines of fur fringing approx. 1in (2.5cm)
apart under the mouth markings using the photo as a
guide for the yarn shades. Brush and trim to the length
required. Continue to add fur fringing all around the
face using the photo as a guide for color markings.
Brush and trim to length required.

It may be beneficial to spray pillow front with
hairspray to keep the yarn in place (optional).

tiger pillow

This bright and regal pillow is a must for any big cat lover. Resembling a giant version of our house cats, this pillow is certainly just that little bit different. Crocheted in single and double crochet stitches, this pattern will enable you to create your own big cat which will be an eye-catching feature in any room.

YARN AND MATERIALS
King Cole Big Value Super Chunky (100% acrylic), super bulky (super chunky) weight yarn, 90yd (81m) per 3½oz (100g) ball
   3 balls of shade 3550 Ginger (A)
   ½ ball of shade 24 Gray (B)
   ½ ball of shade 1758 White (C)
   ½ ball of shade 8 Black (D)

Small amount of pink super bulky (super chunky) weight yarn (E)

Pair of 26mm safety eyes

Small amount of toy fiberfill

14in (35.5cm) round pillow form

Clear nylon fishing line for whiskers (optional, see pattern note)

HOOK AND EQUIPMENT
US J-10 (6mm) crochet hook

Yarn needle

Pins

Stiff brush or pet brush

Hairspray (optional)

FINISHED SIZE
Approx. 16in (40.5cm) diameter

ABBREVIATIONS
See page 142.

PATTERN NOTE
To add 3D whiskers as shown in the photos, please see page 142. Do not add them if you are giving this project to a young child.

PILLOW FRONT AND BACK
(make 2)
Round 1: Using A, ch5, join with a sl st to form a ring.
Round 2: Ch3 (counts as first dc), 11dc in ring, join with a sl st. (*12 sts*)
Round 3: Ch3, 1dc in same dc, 2dc in each dc to end, join with a sl st. (*24 sts*)
Round 4: Ch3, 2dc in next dc, [1dc in next dc, 2dc in next dc] to end, join with a sl st. (*36 sts*)
Round 5: Ch3, 1dc in next dc, 2dc in next dc, [1dc in each of next 2 dc, 2dc in next dc] to end, join with a sl st. (*48 sts*)
Round 6: Ch3, 1dc in each of next 2 dc, 2dc in next dc, [1dc in each of next 3 dc, 2dc in next dc] to end, join with a sl st. (*60 sts*)

Round 7: Ch3, 1dc in each of next 3 dc, 2dc in next dc, [1dc in each of next 4 dc, 2dc in next dc] to end, join with a sl st. (*72 sts*)
Round 8: Ch3, 1dc in each of next 4 dc, 2dc in next dc, [1dc in each of next 5 dc, 2dc in next dc] to end, join with a sl st. (*84 sts*)
Round 9: Ch3, 1dc in each of next 5 dc, 2dc in next dc, [1dc in each of next 6 dc, 2dc in next dc] to end, join with a sl st. (*96 sts*)
Round 10: Ch3, 1dc in each of next 6 dc, 2dc in next dc, [1dc in each of next 7 dc, 2dc in next dc] to end, join with a sl st. (*108 sts*)
Fasten off.

SNOUT

Round 1: Using A, ch4, join with a sl st to form a ring.
Round 2: Ch1 (counts as first sc), 7sc in ring, join with a sl st. (*8 sts*)
Round 3: Ch1, 1sc in same sc, 2sc in each sc to end, join with a sl st. (*16 sts*)
Round 4: Ch1, 1sc in next sc, 1sc in each sc to end, join with a sl st.
Round 5: Ch1, 2sc in next sc, [1sc in next sc, 2sc in next sc] to end, join with a sl st. (*24 sts*)
Round 6: Ch1, 1sc in each of next 2 sc, 2sc in next sc, [1sc in each of next 3 sc, 2sc in next sc] to end, join with a sl st. (*30 sts*)
Round 7: Ch1, 1sc in next sc, 1sc in each sc to end, join with a sl st.
Round 8: Ch1, 1sc in each of next 3 sc, 2sc in next sc, [1sc in each of next 4 sc, 2sc in next sc] to end, join with a sl st. (*36 sts*)
Round 9: Ch1, 1sc in each of next 4 sc, 2sc in next sc, [1sc in each of next 5 sc, 2sc in next sc] to end, join with a sl st. (*42 sts*)
Rounds 10 and 11: Ch1, 1sc in next sc, 1sc in each sc to end, join with a sl st.
Cont working on next 5 sts only to form bridge of snout.
Rows 1–6: Ch1, 1sc in each of next 4 sc, turn. (*5 sts*)
Row 7: Ch1, 1sc in same sc, 1sc in each of next 3 sc, 2sc in next sc. (*7 sts*)
Rows 8 and 9: Ch1, 1sc in next sc, 1sc in each sc to end.
Fasten off.

INNER EARS

(make 2)
Row 1: Using B, ch6.
Row 2: 1sc in 2nd ch from hook (missed ch does not count as sc), 1sc in each ch to end. (*5 sts*)
Row 3: Ch1 (counts as first sc), 1sc in same sc, 1sc in each sc to end. (*6 sts*)
Row 4. Ch1, 1sc in same sc, 1sc in each sc to end. (*7 sts*)
Row 5: Ch1, 1sc in same sc, 1sc in each sc to end. (*8 sts*)
Row 6: Ch1, 1sc in same sc, 1sc in each sc to end. (*9 sts*)
Row 7: Ch1, 1sc in same sc, 1sc in each sc to end. (*10 sts*)
Rows 8 and 9: Ch1, 1sc in next sc, 1sc in each sc to end.
Row 10: Sc2tog, 1sc in each sc to last 2 sc, sc2tog. (*8 sts*)
Fasten off.

OUTER EARS

(make 2)
Row 1: Using A, ch6.
Row 2: 1sc in 2nd ch from hook (missed ch does not count as sc), 1sc in each ch to end. (*5 sts*)
Row 3: Ch1 (counts as first sc), 1sc in same sc, 1sc in each sc to end. (*6 sts*)
Row 4: Ch1, 1sc in same sc, 1sc in each sc to end. (*7 sts*)
Row 5: Ch1, 1sc in same sc, 1sc in each sc to end. (*8 sts*)
Row 6: Ch1, 1sc in same sc, 1sc in each sc to end. (*9 sts*)
Row 7: Ch1, 1sc in same sc, 1sc in each sc to end. (*10 sts*)
Rows 8 and 9: Ch1, 1sc in next sc, 1sc in each sc to end.
Row 10: Sc2tog, 1sc in each sc to last 2 sc, sc2tog. (*8 sts*)
Fasten off.

EYE SURROUNDS

(make 2)

Round 1: Using D, ch4, join with a sl st to form a ring.

Round 2: Ch1 (counts as first sc), 9sc in ring, join with a sl st. (*10 sts*)

Fasten off.

TO MAKE UP

Place the back and front pieces of the pillow with right sides together. Using A, work a single crochet seam (see page 140) around, leaving an opening of approx. 6in (15cm). Turn right side out.

Lay the snout just below the center of the pillow. Pull the center top up slightly and push the bottom of the snout against the pillow to give a triangular shape, pinning in position as you go. When you are happy with the shape, sew the bottom piece flat to the pillow. Stuff the rest of the snout firmly. Using D, embroider the mouth markings and a stripe under the nose. Using E, embroider the nose using the photograph as a guide.

Insert the post of each eye into an eye surround and secure with the safety back. Clip off any surplus post. Sew the eyes to the pillow, using the photo as a guide for positioning.

Place an inner ear on top of an outer ear. Using A, work a single crochet seam around all sides to join both pieces together. Repeat for the other ears, then sew the ears to the top of the pillow using the photos as a guide for positioning.

Adding the fur

Adding the fur on the face can be done in two ways, either with a crochet hook (see page 141) or by threading each strand through with a yarn needle and then tying the ends in a knot close to the fabric. The needle is better for getting into small areas, such as around the eyes. Follow the photos for color placement of the fur.

Cut lengths of yarn approx. 6in (15cm) long. Add two lines of fur fringing approx. 1in (2.5cm) apart under the mouth markings. Continue to add fur all around the face, following the photo for the color markings. Brush and trim to the length required.

It may be beneficial to spray pillow front with hairspray to keep the yarn in place (optional).

The loyal Ragdoll cat has been a family favorite for many years.
Why not have this elegant, happy face crocheted into a pillow
that will sit on any couch or bed?

ragdoll pillow

YARN AND MATERIALS
King Cole Big Value Super Chunky (100% acrylic), super bulky (super chunky) weight yarn, 90yd (81m) per 3½oz (100g) ball
  4 balls of Champagne shade 12 (A)

Small amount black bulky (chunky) weight yarn (B)

Pair of 24mm cat safety eyes

24mm pink cat safety nose

Small amount of toy fiberfill

14in (35.5cm) round pillow form

HOOK AND EQUIPMENT
US J-10 (6mm) crochet hook

Yarn needle

Stiff brush or pet brush

Hairspray (optional)

FINISHED SIZE
Approx. 15in (38cm) diameter

ABBREVIATIONS
See page 142.

PATTERN NOTE
To add 3D whiskers as shown in the photos, please see page 142. Do not add them if you are giving this project to a young child.

PILLOW FRONT AND BACK

(make 2)
Round 1: Using A, ch5, join with a sl st to form a ring.
Round 2: Ch3 (counts as first dc), 11dc in ring, join with a sl st. (*12 sts*)
Round 3: Ch3, 1dc in same dc, 2dc in each dc to end, join with a sl st. (*24 sts*)
Round 4: Ch3, 2dc in next dc, [1dc in next dc, 2dc in next dc] to end, join with a sl st. (*36 sts*)
Round 5: Ch3, 1dc in next dc, 2dc in next dc, [1dc in each of next 2 dc, 2dc in next dc] to end, join with a sl st. (*48 sts*)
Round 6: Ch3, 1dc in each of next 2 dc, 2dc in next dc, [1dc in each of next 3 dc, 2dc in next dc] to end, join with a sl st. (*60 sts*)
Round 7: Ch3, 1dc in each of next 3 dc, 2dc in next dc, [1dc in each of next 4 dc, 2dc in next dc] to end, join with a sl st. (*72 sts*)
Round 8: Ch3, 1dc in each of next 4 dc, 2dc in next dc, [1dc in each of next 5 dc, 2dc in next dc] to end, join with a sl st. (*84 sts*)

Round 9: Ch3, 1dc in each of next 5 dc, 2dc in next dc, [1dc in each of next 6 dc, 2dc in next dc] to end, join with a sl st. (*96 sts*)
Fasten off.

SNOUT

Round 1: Using A, ch8.
Round 2: 1sc in 2nd ch from hook (missed ch does not count as sc), 1sc in each ch to last ch, 3sc in last ch, working along bottom of chain, 1sc in each ch to end, 1sc in end of row, join with a sl st. (*16 sts*)
Round 3: Ch1 (counts as first sc), 1sc in each of next 5 sc, [2sc in next sc] twice, 1sc in each of next 6 sc, [2sc in next sc] twice, join with a sl st. (*20 sts*)
Rounds 4–6: Ch1, 1sc in next sc, 1sc in each sc to end, join with a sl st.
Round 7: Ch1, 1sc in each of the next 7 sc, [2sc in next sc] twice, 1sc in each of next 8 sc, [2sc in next sc] twice, join with a sl st. (*24 sts*)

Round 8: Ch1, 1sc in next sc, 1sc in each sc to end, join with a sl st.
Sl st to center of snout.
Fasten off, leaving a length of yarn for forming snout.

BASE OF SNOUT
Row 1: Using A, ch3.
Row 2: 2sc in 2nd ch from hook (missed ch does not count as sc), 1sc in next sc. (*3 sts*)
Row 3: Ch1 (counts as first sc), 1sc in same sc, 1sc in each sc to end. (*4 sts*)
Row 4: Ch1, 1sc in same sc, 1sc in each sc to end. (*5 sts*)
Row 5: Ch1, 1sc in same sc, 1sc in each sc to end. (*6 sts*)
Fasten off.

EARS
(make 4)
Row 1: Using A, ch2.
Row 2: 1sc in 2nd ch from hook (missed ch does not count as sc). (*1 st*)
Row 3: Ch1 (counts as first sc), 1sc in same sc. (*2 sts*)
Row 4: Ch1, 1sc in same sc, 1sc in each sc to end. (*3 sts*)
Row 5: Ch1, 1sc in same sc, 1sc in each sc to end. (*4 sts*)
Row 6: Ch1, 1sc in same sc, 1sc in each sc to end. (*5 sts*)
Row 7: Ch1, 1sc in same sc, 1sc in each sc to end. (*6 sts*)
Row 8: Ch1, 1sc in same sc, 1sc in each sc to end. (*7 sts*)
Row 9: Ch1, 1sc in same sc, 1sc in each sc to end. (*8 sts*)
Row 10: Ch1, 1sc in same sc, 1sc in each sc to end. (*9 sts*)
Row 11: Ch1, 1sc in same sc, 1sc in each sc to end. (*10 sts*)
Fasten off.

TO MAKE UP
Place front and back with right sides together. Using A, work a single crochet seam (see page 140) around, leaving an opening of approx. 6in (15cm). Turn right side out.

To form the two puffed parts of the snout, stuff the snout lightly then wind the yarn end around the center and secure firmly at the back with a stitch. Using B, embroider mouth markings onto the snout. Push the post of the safety nose through the crochet above the mouth marking and secure with the back, then clip off any excess post. Sew the snout to the front of the pillow. Slightly stuff the base of the snout and sew in position, using the photo as a guide.

Add the safety eyes, using the photo as a guide for positioning, and secure with the safety backs (see page 141).

Insert the pillow form and sew the gap closed.

Place one ear on top of another ear and using A work a single crochet seam through both layers to join. Sew the ears to the top of the head.

Adding the fur
Adding the fur on the face can be done in two ways, either with a crochet hook (see page 141) or by threading each strand through with a yarn needle and then tying the ends into a knot close to the fabric. The needle is better for getting into small areas, such as around the eyes.

Cut A into approx. 7in (18cm) lengths. Starting at the top of the snout, add a line of fur fringe above the snout approx. 1in (2.5cm) wide. Add more lines approx. 2in (5cm) apart until the top of the pillow is covered.

Continue with the rest of the face by starting at the snout and working lines of fringe approx. 2in (5cm) apart outward to the edge of the pillow until the whole front of the pillow is covered. Brush the fringe all around for the fluffy effect and trim to length required.

It may be beneficial to spray the pillow front lightly with hairspray to keep the yarn in place (optional).

CHAPTER 2
home décor

SKILL RATING ● ● ○

YARN AND MATERIALS
King Cole Super Yummy (100% polyester), super bulky (super chunky) weight yarn, 44yd (40m) per 3½oz (100g) ball
    8 balls of shade 4873 Silver (A)
    1 ball of shade 4875 Baby Pink (B)
    1oz (30g) of shade 4874 Ice White (C)

Length of bulky (chunky) yarn in white (D)

Length of bulky (chunky) yarn in black (E)

Length of bulky (chunky) yarn in pink (F)

Length of light worsted (DK) yarn in black (G)

HOOK AND EQUIPMENT
US size L-11 (8mm) crochet hook

Stitch markers

Yarn needle

FINISHED SIZE
Approx. 29in (74cm) diameter (excluding ears)

ABBREVIATIONS
See page 142.

PATTERN NOTE
It is advisable to use stitch markers to identify the beginning of each round.
The Super Yummy yarn can fray very easily at either end. It is recommended that the fluff is pulled away from the cotton for the first 2in (5cm). This produces a short length of the cotton that can be sewn into the work to secure in place. To fasten off in this yarn the same procedure is used.

Brighten up any bedroom with this circular sleeping cat rug. Crocheted in rounds with super soft Yummy yarn, using single crochet, it's a quick and easy project for all skill levels.

sleeping cat rug

MAIN RUG
Round 1: Using A, ch5, join with a sl st to form a ring.
Round 2: Ch1 (counts as first sc), 7sc in ring, join with a sl st. (*8 sts*)
Round 3: Ch1, 1sc in same sc, 2sc in each sc to end, join with a sl st. (*16 sts*)
Round 4: Ch1, 2sc in next sc, [1sc in next sc, 2sc in next sc] to end, join with a sl st. (*24 sts*)
Round 5: Ch1, 1sc in next sc, 2sc in next sc, [1sc in each of next 2 sc, 2sc in next sc] to end, join with a sl st. (*32 sts*)
Round 6: Ch1, 1sc in each of next 2 sc, 2sc in next sc, [1sc in each of next 3 sc, 2sc in next sc] to end. (*40 sts*)
Round 7: Ch1, 1sc in each of next 3 sc, 2sc in next sc, [1sc in each of next 4 sc, 2sc in next sc] to end. (*48 sts*)
Round 8: Ch1, 1sc in each of next 4 sc, 2sc in next sc, [1sc in each of next 5 sc, 2sc in next sc] to end. (*56 sts*)
Round 9: Ch1, 1sc in each of next 5 sc, 2sc in next sc, [1sc in each of next 6 sc, 2sc in next sc] to end. (*64 sts*)
Round 10: Ch1, 1sc in each of next 6 sc, 2sc in next sc, [1sc in each of next 7 sc, 2sc in next sc] to end. (*72 sts*)
Round 11: Ch1, 1sc in each of next 7 sc, 2sc in next sc, [1sc in each of next 8 sc, 2sc in next sc] to end. (*80 sts*)
Round 12: Ch1, 1sc in each of next 8 sc, 2sc in next sc, [1sc in each of next 9 sc, 2sc in next sc] to end. (*88 sts*)
Round 13: Ch1, 1sc in each of next 9 sc, 2sc in next sc, [1sc in each of next 10 sc, 2sc in next sc] to end. (*96 sts*)
Round 14: Ch1, 1sc in each of next 10 sc, 2sc in next sc, [1sc in each of next 11 sc, 2sc in next sc] to end. (*104 sts*)
Round 15: Ch1, 1sc in each of next 11 sc, 2sc in next sc, [1sc in each of next 12 sc, 2sc in next sc] to end. (*112 sts*)
Round 16: Ch1, 1sc in each of next 12 sc, 2sc in next sc, [1sc in each of next 13 sc, 2sc in next sc] to end. (*120 sts*)
Round 17: Ch1, 1sc in each of next 13 sc, 2sc in next sc, [1sc in each of next 14 sc, 2sc in next sc] to end. (*128 sts*)

SNOUT

Round 1: Using C, ch13.

Round 2: 1sc in 2nd ch from hook (missed ch does not count as sc), 1sc in each ch to last ch, 3sc in last ch, working along bottom of chain, 1sc in each ch to end, 1sc in end of row, join with a sl st. (*26 sts*)

Round 3: Ch1 (counts as first sc), 1sc in each of next 10 sc, [2sc in next sc] twice, 1sc in each of next 11 sc, [2sc in next sc] twice, join with a sl st. (*30 sts*)
Fasten off.

BASE OF SNOUT

Row 1: Using C, ch4.

Row 2: 1sc in 2nd ch from hook (missed ch does not count as sc), 1sc in each ch to end. (*3 sts*)

Row 3: Ch1 (counts as first sc), 1sc in same st, 1sc in each sc to end. (*4 sts*)

Row 4: Ch1, 1sc in same st, 1sc in each sc to end. (*5 sts*)

Row 5: Ch1, 1sc in same st, 1sc in each sc to end. (*6 sts*)
Fasten off.

INNER EARS

(make 2)

Row 1: Using B, ch2.

Row 2: 1sc in 2nd ch from hook (missed ch does not count as sc). (*1 st*)

Row 3: Ch1 (counts as first sc), 1sc in same st. (*2 sts*)

Row 4: Ch1, 1sc in same st, 1sc in each sc to end. (*3 sts*)

Row 5: Ch1, 1sc in same st, 1sc in each sc to end. (*4 sts*)

Row 6: Ch1, 1sc in same st, 1sc in each sc to end. (*5 sts*)

Row 7: Ch1, 1sc in same st, 1sc in each sc to end. (*6 sts*)

Row 8: Ch1, 1sc in same st, 1sc in each sc to end. (*7 sts*)

Row 9: Ch1, 1sc in same st, 1sc in each sc to end. (*8 sts*)

Row 10: Ch1, 1sc in same st, 1sc in each sc to end. (*9 sts*)

Row 11: Ch1, 1sc in same st, 1sc in each sc to end. (*10 sts*)

Row 12: Ch1, 1sc in same st, 1sc in each sc to end. (*11 sts*)

Row 13: Ch1, 1sc in same st, 1sc in each sc to end. (*12 sts*)
Fasten off.

Round 18: Ch1, 1sc in each of next 14 sc, 2sc in next sc, [1sc in each of next 15 sc, 2sc in next sc] to end. (*136 sts*)

Round 19: Ch1, 1sc in each of next 15 sc, 2sc in next sc, [1sc in each of next 16 sc, 2sc in next sc] to end. (*144 sts*)

Round 20: Ch1, 1sc in each of next 16 sc, 2sc in next sc, [1sc in each of next 17 sc, 2sc in next sc] to end. (*152 sts*)

Round 21: Ch1, 1sc in each of next 17 sc, 2sc in next sc, [1sc in each of next 18 sc, 2sc in next sc] to end. (*160 sts*)

Round 22: Ch1, 1sc in each of next 18 sc, 2sc in next sc, [1sc in each of next 19 sc, 2sc in next sc] to end. (*168 sts*)

Round 23: Ch1, 1sc in each of next 19 sc, 2sc in next sc, [1sc in each of next 20 sc, 2sc in next sc] to end. (*176 sts*)

Round 24: Ch1, 1sc in each of next 20 sc, 2sc in next sc, [1sc in each of next 21 sc, 2sc in next sc] to end. (*184 sts*)

Round 25: Ch1, 1sc in each of next 21 sc, 2sc in next sc, [1sc in each of next 22 sc, 2sc in next sc] to end. (*192 sts*)
Fasten off.

OUTER EARS

(make 2)

Row 1: Using A, ch2.

Row 2: 1sc in 2nd ch from hook (missed ch does not count as sc). (*1 st*)

Row 3: Ch1 (counts as first sc), 1sc in same st. (*2 sts*)

Row 4: Ch1, 1sc in same st, 1sc in each sc to end. (*3 sts*)

Row 5: Ch1, 1sc in same st, 1sc in each sc to end. (*4 sts*)

Row 6: Ch1, 1sc in same st, 1sc in each sc to end. (*5 sts*)

Row 7: Ch1, 1sc in same st, 1sc in each sc to end. (*6 sts*)

Row 8: Ch1, 1sc in same st, 1sc in each sc to end. (*7 sts*)

Row 9: Ch1, 1sc in same st, 1sc in each sc to end. (*8 sts*)

Row 10: Ch1, 1sc in same st, 1sc in each sc to end. (*9 sts*)

Row 11: Ch1, 1sc in same st, 1sc in each sc to end. (*10 sts*)

Row 12: Ch1, 1sc in same st, 1sc in each sc to end. (*11 sts*)

Row 13: Ch1, 1sc in same st, 1sc in each sc to end. (*12 sts*)

Fasten off.

TO MAKE UP

Lay the rug on a flat surface to make it easier to work.

Place an inner ear on top of an outer ear and, using A, work a single crochet seam (see page 140) all around, with 2sc in each corner, to join both pieces together. Rep for second set of ears. Pin the ears in the positions required at the top of the rug and sew in place.

To form the two parts of the snout, join a length of D to the center top at the back and slightly gather it through the center to the bottom. Pin the base of the snout to the center bottom edge of the main snout and sew in place using D. Join C again and work one round of single crochet all around the whole snout.

Fasten off.

Using B, embroider the nose onto the snout. Using F, embroider mouth markings. Using G, embroider the whiskers in straight stitch (see page 141) in the positions required. Pin the snout onto the center of rug and sew in place.

Using E, embroider the closed eyes. Sew in any yarn ends (see page 139).

What a cozy blanket to warm you up on a chilly evening! This design is crocheted in the popular waffle stitch to give it extra warmth. With the cat silhouette and setting sun, it would make a great gift for any cat lover. Why not make the matching pillow on page 13?

sunset silhouette lap blanket

SKILL RATING ● ● ○

YARN AND MATERIALS
King Cole Safari Chunky (100% acrylic), bulky (chunky) weight yarn, 311yd (285m) per 5¼oz (150g) ball
   6 balls of shade 5005 Sunset (A)

King Cole Moments DK (100% polyester), light worsted (DK) weight yarn, 98yd (90m) per 1¾oz (50g) ball
   2 balls of shade 474 Black (B)

King Cole Cuddles Chunky (100% polyester), bulky (chunky) weight yarn, 136yd (125m) per 1¾oz (50g) ball
   ¾oz (20g) of shade 3821 Sunflower (C)

HOOK AND EQUIPMENT
US H-8 (5mm) crochet hook

Stitch marker

Yarn needle

FINISHED SIZE
Approx. 26 x 41in (66 x 104cm)

ABBREVIATIONS
See page 142.

SPECIAL ABBREVIATION
FPdc (front post double crochet): a double crochet worked by inserting your hook around the post of the next stitch from front to back to front, rather than in the top two loops of a stitch as you normally would

MAIN BLANKET
Row 1: Using A, ch91.
Row 2: 1dc in 3rd ch from hook (missed 2 ch do not count as dc), 1dc in each ch to end. (*89 sts*)
Row 3 (RS): Ch3 (counts as first dc), 1dc in next st, [1FPdc in next st, 1dc in each of next 2 sts] to end.
Row 4 (WS): Ch3, 1FPdc in next st, 1dc in next st, [1FPdc in each of next 2 sts, 1dc in next st] to last 2 sts, 1FPdc in next st, 1dc in last st.
Rep Rows 3 and 4 a further 35 times, then rep Row 3 once.
Do not turn, do not fasten off.

Edging
Continue to work around blanket, starting at corner where last row ended.
Round 1: Ch1, [7dc in end of next square, 1sc in end of next square] to end, join with a sl st.
Fasten off.

CAT FACE
Round 1: Using two strands of B held together, ch4, join with a sl st to form a ring.
Round 2: Ch1 (counts as first sc), 7sc in ring, join with a sl st. (*8 sts*)
Round 3: Ch1, 1sc in same sc, 2sc in each sc to end, join with a sl st. (*16 sts*)
Round 4: Ch1, 2sc in next sc, [1sc in next sc, 2sc in next sc] to end, join with a sl st. (*24 sts*)
Round 5: Ch1, 1sc in next sc, 2sc in next sc, [1sc in each of next 2 sc, 2sc in next sc] to end, join with a sl st. (*32 sts*)
Round 6: Ch1, 1sc in each of next 2 sc, 2sc in next sc, [1sc in each of next 3 sc, 2sc in next sc] to end, join with a sl st. (*40 sts*)
Round 7: Ch1, 1sc in each of next 3 sc, 2sc in next sc, [1sc in each of next 4 sc, 2sc in next sc] to end, join with a sl st. (*48 sts*)
Round 8: Ch1, 1sc in each of next 4 sc, 2sc in next sc, [1sc in each of next 5 sc, 2sc in next sc] to end, join with a sl st. (*56 sts*)
Fasten off.

EARS

(make 2)

Row 1: Using two strands of B held together, ch2.

Row 2: 1sc in 2nd ch from hook (missed ch does not count as sc). (*1 st*)

Row 3: Ch1 (counts as first sc), 1sc in same st. (*2 sts*)

Row 4: Ch1, 1sc in same st, 1sc in each sc to end. (*3 sts*)

Row 5: Ch1, 1sc in same st, 1sc in each sc to end. (*4 sts*)

Row 6: Ch1, 1sc in same st, 1sc in each sc to end. (*5 sts*)

Row 7: Ch1, 1sc in same st, 1sc in each sc to end. (*6 sts*)

Row 8: Ch1, 1sc in same st, 1sc in each sc to end. (*7 sts*)

Row 9: Ch1, 1sc in next sc, 1sc in each sc to end.
Fasten off.

BODY

Row 1: Using two strands of B held together, ch11.

Row 2: 1sc in 2nd ch from hook (missed ch does not count as sc), 1sc in each ch to end. (*10 sts*)

Row 3: Ch1 (counts as first sc), 1sc in same sc, 1sc in each sc to end. (*11 sts*)

Row 4: Ch1, 1sc in same sc, 1sc in each sc to end. (*12 sts*)

Row 5: Ch1, 1sc in same sc, 1sc in each sc to end. (*13 sts*)

Row 6: Ch1, 1sc in same sc, 1sc in each sc to end. (*14 sts*)

Row 7: Ch1, 1sc in same sc, 1sc in each sc to end. (*15 sts*)

Row 8: Ch1, 1sc in same sc, 1sc in each sc to end. (*16 sts*)

Row 9: Ch1, 1sc in same sc, 1sc in each sc to end. (*17 sts*)

Row 10: Ch1, 1sc in same sc, 1sc in each sc to end. (*18 sts*)

Row 11: Ch1, 1sc in same sc, 1sc in each sc to end. (*19 sts*)

Row 12: Ch1, 1sc in same sc, 1sc in each sc to end. (*20 sts*)

Rows 13–25: Ch1, 1sc in next sc, 1sc in each sc to end.

Row 26: Sc2tog, 1sc in each sc to last 2 sc, sc2tog. (*18 sts*)

Row 27: Sc2tog, 1sc to each sc to last 2 sc, sc2tog. (*16 sts*)

Row 28: Ch1, 1sc in next sc, 1sc in each sc to end. Fasten off.

TAIL

Row 1: Using two strands of B held together, ch5.

Row 2: 1sc in 2nd ch from hook (missed ch does not count as sc), 1sc in each ch to end. (*4 sts*)

Row 3: Ch1 (counts as first sc), 1sc in next sc, 1sc in each sc to end. Rep Row 3 until work measures 6in (15cm). Fasten off.

SETTING SUN

Round 1: Using C, ch4, join with a sl st to form a ring.

Round 2: Ch1 (counts as first sc), 7sc in ring, join with a sl st to first sc. (*8 sts*)

Round 3: Ch1, 1sc in same sc, 2sc in each sc to end, join with a sl st. (*16 sts*)

Round 4: Ch1, 2sc in next sc, [1sc in next sc, 2sc in next sc] to end, join with a sl st. (*24 sts*)

Round 5: Ch1, 1sc in next sc, 2sc in next sc, [1sc in each of next 2 sc, 2sc in next sc] to end, join with a sl st. (*32 sts*)

Round 6: Ch1, 1sc in each of next 2 sc, 2sc in next sc, [1sc in each of next 3 sc, 2sc in next sc] to end, join with a sl st. (*40 sts*)

Round 7: Ch1, 1sc in each of next 3 sc, 2sc in next sc, [1sc in each of next 4 sc, 2sc in next sc] to end, join with a sl st. (*48 sts*)

Round 8: Ch1, 1sc in each of next 4 sc, 2sc in next sc, [1sc in each of next 5 sc, 2sc in next sc] to end, join with a sl st. (*56 sts*) Fasten off.

TO MAKE UP

Sew the cat ears to the head using the photo as a guide for positioning, then sew the head to the body. Sew the tail to body.

Pin the cat onto the blanket in the bottom left-hand corner and sew in position. Sew the setting sun onto the blanket at top right.

Sew in any yarn ends (see page 139).

kitten wall plaques

Add charm and character to any wall with these pretty little wall plaques.
Crocheted in super chunky yarn in single crochet stitch throughout,
these plaques can be created in any shade and make perfect gifts.

YARN AND MATERIALS
King Cole Big Value Super Chunky (100% acrylic), super bulky (super chunky) weight yarn, 90yd (81m) per 3½oz (100g) ball
  1 ball each of either:
  Brass shade 3400 (A)
  White shade 1758 (A)
  Gray shade 24 (A)

Small amount of black (or gray for the white cat) light worsted (DK) yarn (B)

5in (13cm) round drum cake board

Pair of 14mm cat safety eyes

12mm pink cat safety nose

Small amount of toy fiberfill

Fabric glue for attaching to cake board

Bow embellishment for decoration (optional)

HOOK AND EQUIPMENT
US H-8 (5mm) crochet hook

Yarn needle

Stiff brush or pet brush

Hairspray (optional)

Pins

Sewing needle and thread (optional)

FINISHED SIZE
6in (15cm) in diameter

ABBREVIATIONS
See page 142.

MAIN PLAQUE
Round 1: Using A, ch4, join with a sl st to form a ring.
Round 2: Ch1 (counts as first sc), 7sc in ring, join with a sl st. (*8 sts*)
Round 3: Ch1, 1sc in same sc, 2sc in each sc to end, join with a sl st. (*16 sts*)
Round 4: Ch1, 2sc in next sc, [1sc in next sc, 2sc in next sc] to end, join with a sl st. (*24 sts*)
Round 5: Ch1, 1sc in next sc, 2sc in next sc, [1sc in each of next 2 sc, 2sc in next sc] to end, join with a sl st. (*32 sts*)
Round 6: Ch1, 1sc in each of next 2 sc, 2sc in next sc, [1sc in each of next 3 sc, 2sc in next sc] to end, join with a sl st. (*40 sts*)
Round 7: Ch1, 1sc in each of next 3 sc, 2sc in next sc, [1sc in each of next 4 sc, 2sc in next sc] to end, join with a sl st. (*48 sts*)
Round 8: Ch1, 1scBLO in next sc, 1scBLO in each sc to end, join with a sl st.
Round 9: Ch1, 1sc in next sc, 1sc in each sc to end, join with a sl st.
Fasten off.

SNOUT

Round 1: Using A, ch6.
Round 2: 1sc in 2nd ch from hook (missed ch does not count as sc), 1sc in each ch to last ch, 3sc in last ch, working along bottom of chain, 1sc in each ch to end, 1sc in end of row, join with a sl st. (*12 sts*)
Round 3: Ch1 (counts as first sc), 1sc in each of next 4 sc, 2sc in next sc, 1sc in each of next 5 sc, 2sc in last sc, join with a sl st. (*14 sts*)
Rounds 4-6: Ch1, 1sc in next sc, 1sc in each sc to end, join with a sl st.
Sl st to center of snout.
Fasten off, leaving a length of yarn for forming snout.

BASE OF SNOUT

Round 1: Using A, ch4, join with a sl st to form a ring.
Round 2: Ch1 (counts as first sc), 9sc in ring, join with a sl st. (*10 sts*)
Fasten off.

EARS

(make 2)
Row 1: Using A, ch2.
Row 2: 1sc in 2nd ch from hook (missed ch does not count as sc). (*1 st*)
Row 3: Ch1 (counts as first sc), 1sc in same sc. (*2 sts*)
Row 4: Ch1, 1sc in same sc, 1sc in next sc. (*3 sts*)
Row 5: Ch1, 1sc in same sc, 1sc in each sc to end. (*4 sts*)
Fasten off.

TO MAKE UP

To form the two puffed parts of the snout, stuff the snout lightly then wind the yarn end around the center, and secure firmly at the back with a stitch. Using B, embroider mouth markings onto the snout. Push the post of the safety nose through the crochet above the mouth marking and secure with the back. Clip off any surplus nose post. Sew the snout to the front of the face. Stuff the base of snout lightly and then sew below the snout.

Add the safety eyes using the photo as a guide for positioning and secure with the backs (see page 141).

Sew the ears to the top of the plaque using the photo as a guide for positioning.

Adding the fur

Adding the fur on the face can be done in two ways, either with a crochet hook (see page 141) or by threading each strand through with a yarn needle and then tying the ends into a knot close to the fabric. The needle is better for getting into small areas, such as around the eyes.

Cut A into 6in (15cm) lengths. Starting at the side of the snout work lines of fur fringe. Repeat on the other side of the snout. Brush and trim to length required. Continue to add fur all around the face, using the photo as a guide. Brush and trim to length required.

When the face is complete, spread glue on the front and sides of the cake board. Lay the back of the face onto the board and press in place. Add pins through the base all around the side of the board to hold in place until the glue has dried. When dry remove the pins.

It may be beneficial to spray the fur lightly with hairspray to keep the yarn in place (optional).

Add any embellishments (optional).

Entertain your friends and family with these unusual big cat paw print drinks coasters. This is a great project for the beginner, and you can create the coasters in any shades you like.

big cat paw print coasters

SKILL RATING ● ● ●

YARN AND MATERIALS
King Cole Big Value Super Chunky (100% acrylic), super bulky (super chunky) weight yarn, 90yd (81m) per 3½oz (100g) ball
  ¼ ball of Brass shade 3400 (A)
  ¼ ball of Champagne shade 12 (B)

HOOK AND EQUIPMENT
US H-8 (5mm) crochet hook

Yarn needle

FINISHED SIZE
Width 4in (10cm)
Length 5in (13cm)

ABBREVIATIONS
See page 142.

PATTERN NOTE
These paw prints can be produced using any of the range of big cat shades—they are a perfect way to use up leftover yarns.

PAW PRINT COASTER

(make 3)

Round 1: Using A, ch4, join with a sl st to form a ring

Round 2: Ch2 (counts as 1hdc), 8hdc in ring, join with a sl st. (*9 sts*)

Round 3: Ch2, 1hdc in same st, 2hdc in each hdc to end, join with a sl st. (*18 sts*)

Join in B.

Round 4: Using B, ch2, 1hdc in same st, 2hdc in each hdc to end, join with a sl st. (*36 sts*)

Round 5: Ch2, (3dc, ch2, sl st) in same st, [miss 2 hdc, (sl st, ch2, 3dc, ch2, sl st) in next st] 3 times (four toe pads), change to A, 1sc in each hdc to end.

Round 6: Using A, working across toe pads only, *1sc in each st around next pad, spike sc (see page 136) between toe pads working into corresponding stitch in Round 3 using photo as a guide; rep from * twice more, 1sc in each st around last pad, sl st in next st.

Fasten off.

Make another three coasters, reversing yarn colors.

TO MAKE UP

Sew in any yarn ends (see page 139).

cat and mouse draft excluder

Who wouldn't want to create this bright and colorful draft excluder with a difference? Crocheted in single crochet stitch throughout, this fun and unique design would be a stand-out feature in any room.

SKILL RATING ● ● ●

YARN AND MATERIALS
King Cole Hedgerow Chunky (100% acrylic), bulky (chunky) weight yarn, 332yd (304m) per 7oz (200g) ball
   1½ balls of shade 5842 Holly Berry (A)

King Cole Big Value Chunky (100% acrylic), bulky (chunky) weight yarn, 167yd (152m) per 3½oz (100g) ball
   ⅛ ball of shade 822 White (B)

King Cole Yummy (100% polyester), bulky (chunky) weight yarn, 131yd (120m) per 3½oz (100g) ball
   Small amount of shade 3477 Champagne (C)

King Cole Big Value DK 50g (100% acrylic), light worsted (DK) weight yarn, 158yd (145m) per 1¾oz (50g) ball
   1 ball of shade 4069 Silver (D)

King Cole Glitz DK (97% acrylic, 5% polyester), light worsted (DK) weight yarn, 317yd (290m) per 1¾oz (50g) ball
   Small amount of shade 4721 Pink (E)

Small amount of black bulky (chunky) weight yarn (F)

Toy fiberfill

Pair of 18mm safety eyes

18mm pink safety nose

Embellishments of your choice

HOOK AND EQUIPMENT
US G-6 (4mm), US H-8 (5mm), and US D (3mm) crochet hooks
Yarn needle

FINISHED LENGTH
33in (84cm)

ABBREVIATIONS
See page 142.

CAT MAIN BODY

Round 1: Using US H-8 (5mm) hook and A, ch4, join with a sl st to form a ring.

Round 2: Ch1 (counts as first sc), 7sc in ring, join with a sl st. (*8 sts*)

Round 3: Ch1, 1sc in same sc, 2sc in each sc to end, join with a sl st. (*16 sts*)

Round 4: Ch1, 2sc in next sc, [1sc in next sc, 2sc in next sc] to end, join with a sl st. (*24 sts*)

Round 5: Ch1, 1sc in next sc, 2sc in next sc, [1sc in each of next 2 sc, 2sc in next sc] to end, join with a sl st. (*32 sts*)

Round 6: Ch1, 1sc in each of next 2 sc, 2sc in next sc, [1sc in each of next 3 sc, 2sc in next sc] to end, join with a sl st. (*40 sts*)

Round 7: Ch1, 1sc in each of next 3 sc, 2sc in next sc, [1sc in each of next 4 sc, 2sc in next sc] to end, join with a sl st. (*48 sts*)

Round 8: Ch1, 1scBLO in next sc, 1scBLO in each sc to end, join with a sl st.

Rounds 9–85: Ch1, 1sc in next sc, 1sc in each sc to end, join with a sl st.

Round 6: Ch1, 1sc in next sc, 2sc in next sc, [1sc in each of next 2 sc, 2sc in next sc] to end, join with a sl st. (*16 sts*)

Rounds 7–24: Ch1, 1sc in next sc, 1sc in each sc to end, join with a sl st.
Fasten off.

CAT HAT AND HEAD

Round 1: Using US H-8 (5mm) hook and B, ch4, join with a sl st to form a ring.

Round 2: Ch1 (counts as first sc), 7sc in ring, join with a sl st. (*8 sts*)

Round 3: Ch1, 1sc in same sc, 2sc in each sc to end, join with a sl st. (*16 sts*)

Round 4: Ch1, 2sc in next sc, [1sc in next sc, 2sc in next sc] to end, join with a sl st. (*24 sts*)

Round 5: Ch1, 1sc in next sc, 2sc in next sc, [1sc in each of next 2 sc, 2sc in next sc] to end, join with a sl st. (*32 sts*)

Round 6: Ch1, 1sc in each of next 2 sc, 2sc in next sc, [1sc in each of next 3 sc, 2sc in next sc] to end, join with a sl st. (*40 sts*)

Round 7: Ch1, 1sc in each of next 3 sc, 2sc in next sc, [1sc in each of next 4 sc, 2sc in next sc] to end, join with a sl st. (*48 sts*)

Round 8: Ch1, 1sc in each of next 4 sc, 2sc in next sc, [1sc in each of next 5 sc, 2sc in next sc] to end, join with a sl st. (*56 sts*)

Round 9: Ch1, 1scBLO in next sc, 1scBLO in each sc to end, join with a sl st. (*56 sts*)

Rounds 10–14: Ch1, 1sc in next sc, 1sc in each sc to end, join with a sl st.

Round 15: Change to A, ch1, 1scBLO in next sc, 1scBLO in each sc to end, join with a sl st.

Rounds 16–20: Ch1, 1sc in next sc, 1sc in each sc to end, join with a sl st.

Round 21: Ch1, 1sc in each of next 4 sc, sc2tog, [1sc in each of next 5 sc, sc2tog] to end, join with a sl st. (*48 sts*)

Round 22: Ch1, 1sc in each of next 3 sc, sc2tog, [1sc in each of next 4 sc, sc2tog] to end, join with a sl st. (*40 sts*)

Round 23: Ch1, 1sc in each of next 2 sc, sc2tog, [1sc in each of next 3 sc, sc2tog] to end, join with a sl st. (*32 sts*)

Round 24: Ch1, 1sc in next sc, 1sc in each sc to end, join with a sl st.

Round 25: Ch1, 1sc in next sc, sc2tog, [1sc in each of next 2 sc, sc2tog] to end, join with a sl st. (*24 sts*)

Round 26: Ch1, 1sc in next sc, 1sc in each sc to end, join with a sl st.

Round 86: Ch1, 1scBLO in each of next 3 sc, sc2togBLO, 1scBLO in each of next 4 sc, sc2togBLO] to end, join with a sl st. (*40 sts*)

Round 87: Ch1, 1sc in each of next 2 sc, sc2tog, [1sc in each of next 3 sc, sc2tog] to end, join with a sl st. (*32 sts*)

Round 88: Ch1, 1sc in next sc, sc2tog, [1sc in each of next 2 sc, sc2tog] to end, join with a sl st. (*24 sts*)

Round 89: Ch1, sc2tog, [1sc in next sc, sc2tog] to end, join with a sl st. (*16 sts*)
Stuff the body firmly.

Round 90: (Sc2tog] to end, join with a sl st. (*8 sts*)
Fasten off, leaving a length of yarn.
Thread end onto needle, gather remaining sts together, fasten off.

CAT FRONT LEGS

(make 2)

Round 1: Using US H-8 (5mm) hook and A, ch4, join with a sl st to form a ring.

Round 2: Ch1 (counts as first sc), 7sc in ring, join with a sl st. (*8 sts*)

Round 3: Ch1, 1sc in next sc, 1sc in each sc to end, join with a sl st.

Round 4: Ch1, 2sc in next sc, [1sc in next sc, 2sc in next sc] to end, join with a sl st. (*12 sts*)

Round 5: Ch1, 1sc in next sc, 1sc in each sc to end, join with a sl st.

Round 27: Ch1, sc2tog, [1sc in next sc, sc2tog] to end, join with a sl st. (*16 sts*)
Fasten off, leaving a length of yarn.

Brim of hat
Using US H-8 (5mm) hook, join B in front loop of center back stitch of Round 14.
Round 1: Ch1, 1sc in next sc, 1sc in each sc to end, join with a sl st. (*56 sts*)
Round 2: Ch3 (counts as first dc), 2dc in next sc, [1dc in next sc, 2dc in next sc] to end, join with a sl st. (*84 sts*)
Fasten off.

CAT SNOUT
Round 1: Using US H-8 (5mm) hook and C, ch6.
Round 2: 1sc in 2nd ch from hook (missed ch does not count as sc), 1sc in each ch to last ch, 3sc in last ch, working along bottom of chain, 1sc in each ch to end, 1sc in end of row, join with a sl st. (*12 sts*)
Round 3: Ch1 (counts as first sc), 1sc in each of next 3 sc, [2sc in next sc] twice, 1sc in each of next 4 sc, [2sc in next sc] twice, join with a sl st. (*16 sts*)
Round 5: Ch1, 1sc in next sc, 1sc in each sc to end, join with a sl st.
Sl st to center of snout.
Fasten off, leaving a length of yarn for forming snout.

CAT BASE OF SNOUT
Row 1: Using US H-8 (5mm) hook and C, ch3.
Row 2: 1sc in 2nd ch from hook (missed ch does not count as sc), 1sc in next ch. (*2 sts*)
Row 3: Ch1 (counts as first sc), 1sc in same sc, 1sc in each sc to end. (*3 sts*)
Row 4: Ch1, 1sc in same sc, 1sc in each sc to end. (*4 sts*)
Row 5: Ch1, 1sc in same sc, 1sc in each sc to end. (*5 sts*)
Fasten off.

CAT EARS
(make 2)
Row 1: Using US H-8 (5mm) hook and A, ch2.
Row 2: 1sc in 2nd ch from hook (missed ch does not count as sc). (*1 st*)
Row 3: Ch1 (counts as first sc), 1sc in same sc. (*2 sts*)
Row 4: Ch1, 1sc in same sc, 1sc in each sc to end. (*3 sts*)
Row 5: Ch1, 1sc in same sc, 1sc in each sc to end. (*4 sts*)
Row 6: Ch1, 1sc in same sc, 1sc in each sc to end. (*5 sts*)
Row 7: Ch1, 1sc in same sc, 1sc in each sc to end. (*6 sts*)
Row 8: Ch1, 1sc in same sc, 1sc in each sc to end. (*7 sts*)
Fasten off.

CAT BACK LEGS
(make 2)
Round 1: Using US H-8 (5mm) hook and A, ch4, join with a sl st to form a ring.
Round 2: Ch1 (counts as first sc), 7sc in ring, join with a sl st. (*8 sts*)
Round 3: Ch1, 1sc in next sc, 1sc in each sc to end, join with a sl st.
Round 4: Ch1, 2sc in next sc, [1sc in next sc, 2sc in next sc] to end, join with a sl st. (*12 sts*)
Rounds 5–15: Ch1, 1sc in next sc, 1sc in each sc to end, join with a sl st.
Fasten off.

CAT TAIL
Round 1: Using US H-8 (5mm) hook and A, ch4, join with a sl st to form a ring.
Round 2: Ch1 (counts as first sc), 7sc in ring, join with a sl st. (*8 sts*)
Round 3: Ch1, 1sc in next sc, 1sc in each sc to end, join with a sl st.
Rep Round 3 until work measures 11in (28cm), adding toy fiberfill as you go.
Fasten off.

CAT COLLAR

Row 1: Using US H-8 (5mm) hook and B, ch31.
Row 2: 1sc in 2nd ch from hook (missed ch does not count as sc), 1sc in each ch to end. (*30 sts*)
Fasten off.

MOUSE HEAD

(make 3)
Round 1: Using US D (3mm) hook and D, ch4, join with a sl st to form a ring.
Round 2: Ch1 (counts as first sc), 5sc in ring, join with a sl st. (*6 sts*)
Rounds 3 and 4: Ch1, 1sc in next sc, 1sc in each sc to end, join with a sl st.
Round 5: Ch1, 2sc in next sc, [1sc in next sc, 2sc in next sc] to end, join with a sl st. (*9 sts*)
Round 6: Ch1, 1sc in next sc, 2sc in next sc, [1sc in each of next 2 sc, 2sc in next sc] to end, join with a sl st. (*12 sts*)
Round 7: Ch1, 2sc in next sc, [1sc in next sc, 2sc in next sc] to end, join with a sl st. (*18 sts*)
Round 8: Ch1, 1sc in next sc, 1sc in each sc to end, join with a sl st.
Round 9: Ch1, sc2tog, [1sc in next sc, sc2tog] to end, join with a sl st. (*12 sts*)
Round 10: Ch1, sc2tog, [1sc in next sc, sc2tog] to end, join with a sl st. (*8 sts*)
Fasten off.

MOUSE INNER EAR

(make 6)
Round 1: Using US D (3mm) hook and E, ch4, join with a sl st to form a ring.
Round 2: Ch1 (counts as first sc), 7sc in ring, join with a sl st. (*8 sts*)
Fasten off.

MOUSE OUTER EAR

(make 6)
Round 1: Using US D (3mm) hook and D, ch4, join with a sl st to form a ring.
Round 2: Ch1, 7sc in ring, join with a sl st. (*8 sts*)
Fasten off.

MOUSE BODY

(make 3)
Round 1: Using US D (3mm) hook and D, ch4, join with a sl st to form a ring.
Round 2: Ch1 (counts as first sc), 7sc in ring, join with a sl st. (*8 sts*)
Round 3: Ch1, 1sc in same sc, 2sc in each sc to end, join with a sl st. (*16 sts*)
Round 4: Ch1, 1sc in each of next 2 sc, 2sc in next sc, [1sc in each of next 3 sc, 2sc in next sc] to end, join with a sl st. (*20 sts*)
Round 5: Ch1, 1sc in each of next 3 sc, 2sc in next sc, [1sc in each of next 4 sc, 2sc in next sc] to end, join with a sl st. (*24 sts*)
Rounds 6-10: Ch1, 1sc in next sc, 1sc in each sc to end, join with a sl st.

Round 11: Ch1, 1sc in each of next 3 sc, sc2tog, [1sc in each of next 4 sc, sc2tog] to end, join with a sl st. (*20 sts*)

Round 12: Ch1, 1sc in each of next 2 sc, sc2tog, [1sc in each of next 3 sc, sc2tog] to end, join with a sl st. (*16 sts*)
Stuff firmly.

Round 13: [Sc2tog] to end, join with a sl st. (*8 sts*)
Fasten off.

MOUSE ARMS
(make 6)
Round 1: Using US D (3mm) hook and D, ch4, join with a sl st to form a ring.
Round 2: Ch1 (counts as first sc), 5sc in ring, join with a sl st. (*6 sts*)
Rounds 3–8: Ch1, 1sc in next sc, 1sc in each sc to end, join with a sl st.
Fasten off.

MOUSE FEET
(make 6)
Round 1: Using US D (3mm) hook and E, ch4, join with a sl st to form a ring.
Round 2: Ch1 (counts as first sc), 5sc in ring, join with a sl st. (*6 sts*)
Rounds 3 and 4: Ch1, 1sc in next sc, 1sc in each sc to end, join with a sl st.
Fasten off.

MOUSE TAIL
(make 3)
Row 1: Using US D (3mm) hook and D, ch13.
Row 2: 1sc in 2nd ch from hook (missed ch does not count as a sc), 1sc in each ch to end. (*12 sts*)
Fasten off, leaving a length of yarn for sewing to body.

TO MAKE UP
Cat
Stuff the top half of the head firmly. Add the safety eyes and secure with the backs (see page 141), using the photo as a guide for positioning. Stuff the remainder of the head firmly and then draw the yarn ends through the remaining stitches and fasten off.

To form the two puffed parts of the snout, stuff the snout lightly then wind the yarn end around the center and secure firmly at the back with a stitch. Using F, embroider mouth markings onto the snout. Push the post of the safety nose through the crochet above the mouth marking and secure with the back. Sew the snout onto the center of the head, using the photo as a guide. Using F, embroider the whiskers in straight

stitch (see page 141) . Sew the base of the snout below the snout. Sew the ears on the top of the hat, using the photo as a guide for positioning. Sew the head onto the body in the position required.

Stuff the front legs and sew on at the front of the body, making sure that the bottom of each leg is in line with the body on the ground. It may be advisable to secure both legs together in the center to hold them together.

Stuff the back legs and sew them to the back of the body, using the photo as a guide. Sew the tail onto the back of the body in the middle, then drape it around the front of the body and secure in place with a few stitches.

Sew the collar around the neck and add any embellishments.

Mouse
Stuff each head.

Using E, oversew a few stitches to form the snout. Using F, embroider the eyes and mouth, using the photo as a guide.

Place each inner ear on top of an outer ear and work a round of single crochet with D to join both pieces together. Fasten off then sew a pair of ears to each mouse head. Sew a head to each body.

Sew a pair of arms to each body, using the photo as a guide. Sew a pair of feet to the bottom of each body. Sew a tail at the base of the back of the body.

Sew the mice to the top of the draft excluder in the positions required and add any embellishments.

SKILL RATING ● ● ○

YARN AND MATERIALS
King Cole Big Value Chunky (100% acrylic), bulky (chunky) weight yarn, 167yd (152m) per 3½oz (100g) ball
  1 ball of Forest shade 3642 (A)

King Cole Velveteen (100% polyester), super bulky (super chunky) weight yarn, 71yd (65m) per 3½oz (100g) ball
  1 ball of Snow shade 6120 (B)

Oddments of bulky (chunky) or light worsted (DK) weight yarn in preferred colors

Small amount of black light worsted (DK) weight yarn (C)

12in (30cm) polystyrene ring

Toy fiberfill

Pair of 18mm cat safety eyes

18mm pink cat safety nose

3 ladybug embellishments (optional)

HOOK AND EQUIPMENT
US H-8 (5mm) crochet hook

Stitch marker

Yarn needle

Pins

Sewing needle and thread

FINISHED SIZE
13in (33cm) in diameter

Abbreviations
See page 142.

PATTERN NOTES
It is advisable to use a stitch marker with the Velveteen yarn. The flowers can be produced from oddments of yarn from your stash because each flower uses very little yarn, enabling you to produce your own individual wreath in your desired shades with as many flowers as required.

Brighten up any wall or door with this stunning wreath and cheeky little cat's face. This pattern enables you to design your own individual wreath by adding as many flowers in any colorways you choose. Crocheted in double and single crochet stitches throughout, it's the perfect project for using up leftover yarns in your stash.

cat flower wreath

MAIN WREATH COVER
Row 1: Using A, ch22.
Row 2: 1hdc in 3rd ch from hook (missed 2 ch do not count as hdc), 1hdc in each ch to end. (*20 sts*)
Row 3: Ch2 (counts as first hdc), 1hdc in next hdc, 1hdc in each hdc to end.
Rep Row 3 until work covers ring when stretched (use pins to stretch in place).
Fasten off, leaving a length of yarn for sewing seam.

HEAD
Round 1: Using B, ch4, join with a sl st to form a ring.
Round 2: Ch1 (counts as first sc), 7sc in ring, join with a sl st. (*8 sts*)
Round 3: Ch1, 1sc in same sc, 2sc in each sc to end, join with a sl st. (*16 sts*)
Round 4: Ch1, 2sc in next sc, [1sc in next sc, 2sc in next sc] to end, join with a sl st. (*24 sts*)
Round 5: Ch1, 1sc in next sc, 1sc in each sc to end, join with a sl st.
Round 6: Ch1, 1sc in each of next 2 sc, 2sc in next sc, [1sc in each of next 3 sc, 2sc in next sc] to end, join with a sl st. (*30 sts*)
Rounds 7–11: Ch1, 1sc in next sc, 1sc in each sc to end, join with a sl st.
Round 12: Ch1, sc2tog, [1sc in next sc, sc2tog] to end, join with a sl st. (*20 sts*)
Round 13: Ch1, 1sc in each of next 2 sc, sc2tog, [1sc in each of next 3 sc, sc2tog] to end, join with a sl st. (*16 sts*)
Round 14: Ch1, 1sc in next sc, sc2tog, [1sc in each of next 2 sc, sc2tog] to end, join with a sl st. (*12 sts*)
Fasten off, leaving a length of yarn.

SNOUT
Round 1: Using B, ch5.
Round 2: 1sc in 2nd ch from hook (missed ch does not count as sc), 1sc in each ch to last ch, 3sc in last ch, working along bottom of chain, 1sc in each ch to end, 1sc in end of row, join with a sl st. (*10 sts*)

Round 3: Ch1 (counts as first sc), 1sc in next sc, 1sc in each sc to end, join with a sl st.
Sl st to center of snout.
Fasten off, leaving a length of yarn for forming snout.

BASE OF SNOUT

Row 1: Using B, ch3.
Row 2: 1sc in 2nd ch from hook (missed ch does not count as sc), 1sc in next ch. (*2 sts*)
Row 3: Ch1 (counts as first sc), 1sc in same sc, 1sc in next sc. (*3 sts*)
Row 4: Ch1, 1sc in same sc, 1sc in each sc to end. (*4 sts*)
Fasten off.
Trim off any excess fur.

EARS

(make 2)
Row 1: Using B, ch2.
Row 2: 1sc in 2nd ch from hook (missed ch does not count as sc). (*1 st*)
Row 3: Ch1 (counts as first sc), 1sc in same sc. (*2 sts*)
Row 4: Ch1, 1sc in same sc, 1sc in next sc. (*3 sts*)
Row 5: Ch1, 1sc in same sc, 1sc in each sc to end. (*4 sts*)
Row 6: Ch1, 1sc in same sc, 1sc in each sc to end. (*5 sts*)
Fasten off.

PAWS

(make 2)

Row 1: Using B, ch4.

Row 2: 1sc in 2nd ch from hook (missed ch does not count as sc), 1sc in each ch to end. (*3 sts*)

Row 3: Ch1 (counts as first sc), 1sc in same sc, 1sc in each sc to end. (*4 sts*)

Rows 4–6: Ch1, 1sc in next sc, 1sc in each sc to end. Fasten off.

FLOWER 1

Round 1: Using first color, ch4, join with a sl st to form a ring.

Round 2: Ch1 (counts as first sc), 7sc in ring, join with a sl st. (*8 sts*)

Fasten off first color, join second color (or continue with first color for solid color flower).

Round 3: Ch2, (2dc, ch2, sl st) in same st (first petal), [(sl st, ch2, 2dc, ch2, sl st) in next sc] to end. (*8 petals*) Fasten off.

FLOWER 2

Round 1: Using first color, ch4, join with a sl st to form a ring.

Round 2: Ch1 (counts as first sc), 7sc in ring, join with a sl st. (*8 sts*)

Fasten off first color, join second color.

Round 3: Ch2, (2dc, ch2, sl st) in same st (first petal), [(sl st, ch2, 2dc, ch2, sl st) in next sc] to end. (*8 petals*)

Fasten off second color, join third color.

Round 4: Ch1, 1sc in each st and ch around, join with a sl st.

Fasten off.

FLOWER 3

Round 1: Using first color, ch4, join with a sl st to form a ring.

Round 2: Ch1 (counts as first sc), 7sc in ring, join with a sl st. (*8 sts*)

Fasten off first color, join second color.

Round 3: Ch1, 1sc in same sc, 2sc in each sc to end. (*16 sts*)

Fasten off second color, join third color.

Round 4: Ch3, (1dc, ch3, sl st) in same st (first petal), [(sl st, ch3, 1dc, ch3, sl st) in next st] to end. (*16 petals*) Fasten off.

FLOWER 4

Round 1: Using first color, ch5, join with a sl st to form a ring.

Fasten off first color, join second color.

Round 2: Ch5, 1sc in same ch (at base of 5 ch), [(sl st, ch5, 1sc) in next ch] to end.

Fasten off.

TO MAKE UP

Wreath

Sew the seams of the cover all around the wreath, enclosing the ring, plus the seam to join the short ends. Remove all pins.

Arrange all the flowers on the wreath to cover it, following the photo as a guide and pin in place to secure. Sew each flower in place.

Cat

Partly stuff the head to give shape.

To form the two puffed parts of the snout, stuff the snout lightly then wind the yarn end around the center and secure firmly at the back with a stitch. Using C, embroider mouth markings onto the snout. Push the post of the safety nose through the crochet above the mouth marking and secure with the back. Sew the snout to the front of the head. Sew the base of snout below the snout.

Add the safety eyes using the photo as a guide for positioning and secure with the backs (see page 141). Continue stuffing the head until firm. Thread the yarn end onto a needle, gather the remaining sts together and fasten off. Sew the ears to the head using the photo as a guide for positioning.

Sew the head to the wreath, securing all around.

Sew the paws below the head, adding a small amount of stuffing.

Add any embellishments (optional).

lion wall plaque

Showcase this unusual wall hanging on any wall to create a statement piece for your home. The base of this regal-looking lion is crocheted in double crochet stitch, and then the mane is added and brushed.

SKILL RATING ● ● ○

YARN AND MATERIALS
King Cole Big Value Super Chunky (100% acrylic), super bulky (super chunky) weight yarn, 90yd (81m) per 3½oz (100g) ball
- 2 balls of Latte shade 3490 (A)
- 1 ball of Brown shade 31 (B)
- Small amount of White shade 1758 (C)

Small amount of black bulky (chunky) weight yarn (D)

12in (30cm) round drum cake board

24mm safety eye

24mm black safety nose

HOOK AND EQUIPMENT
US I-9 (5.5mm) crochet hook

Yarn needle

Stiff brush or pet brush

Hairspray (optional)

Fabric glue

FINISHED SIZE
13in (33cm) in diameter

ABBREVIATIONS
See page 142.

MAIN BASE
Round 1: Using A, ch5, join with a sl st to form a ring.

Round 2: Ch3 (counts as first dc), 11dc in ring, join with a sl st. (*12 sts*)

Round 3: Ch3, 1dc in same dc, 2dc in each dc to end, join with a sl st. (*24 sts*)

Round 4: Ch3, 2dc in next dc, [1dc in next dc, 2dc in next dc] to end, join with a sl st. (*36 sts*)

Round 5: Ch3, 1dc in next dc, 2dc in next dc, [1dc in each of next 2 dc, 2dc in next dc] to end, join with a sl st. (*48 sts*)

Round 6: Ch3, 1dc in each of next 2 dc, 2dc in next dc, [1dc in each of next 3 dc, 2dc in next dc] to end, join with a sl st. (*60 sts*)

Round 7: Ch3, 1dc in each of next 3 dc, 2dc in next dc, [1dc in each of next 4 dc, 2dc in next dc] to end, join with a sl st. (*72 sts*)

Round 8: Ch3, 1dc in each of next 4 dc, 2dc in next dc, [1dc in each of next 5 dc, 2dc in next dc] to end, join with a sl st. (*84 sts*)

Round 9: Ch3, 1dc in each of next 5 dc, 2dc in next dc, [1dc in each of next 6 dc, 2dc in next dc] to end, join with a sl st. (*96 sts*)
Fasten off.

SNOUT

Round 1: Using A, ch5, join with a sl st to form a ring.
Round 2: Ch3 (counts as first dc), 11dc in ring, join with a sl st. (*12 sts*)
Round 3: Ch3, 1dc in same dc, 2dc in each dc to end, join with a sl st. (*24 sts*)
Round 4: Ch3, 2dc in next dc, [1dc in next dc, 2dc in next dc] to end, join with a sl st. (*36 sts*)
Round 5: Ch3, [1dc in each of next 2 dc, 2dc in next dc] 3 times, 1dc in next dc, leave remaining sts unworked. (*14 sts*)
Fasten off.

EYE SURROUND

Round 1: Using D, ch5, join with a sl st to form a ring.
Round 2: Ch3 (counts as first dc), 11dc in ring, join with a sl st. (*12 sts*)
Fasten off.

EAR

(make 2)
Row 1: Using A, ch6.
Row 2: 1sc in 2nd ch from hook (missed ch does not count as sc), 1sc in each ch to end. (*5 sts*)
Row 3: Ch1 (counts as first sc), 1sc in same sc, 1sc in each sc to end. (*6 sts*)
Row 4: Ch1, 1sc in same sc, 1sc in each sc to end. (*7 sts*)
Row 5: Ch1, 1sc in same sc, 1sc in each sc to end. (*8 sts*)
Row 6: Ch1, 1sc in same sc, 1sc in each sc to end. (*9 sts*)
Row 7: Ch1, 1sc in same sc, 1sc in each sc to end. (*10 sts*)
Fasten off.

TO MAKE UP

Place the snout on top of the main base, so it overlaps at one edge, using the photo as a guide for placement. The front edge of the snout will extend out to be folded over to the back of the cake base when everything is assembled. Sew around the snout to join it to the main base where they overlap. Using B, mark a curved line on the snout to indicate where the mane separates from the face fur.

Push the safety eye through the eye surround and secure with the back (see page 141), then clip off the surplus eye post so the work will lay flat. Using D, embroider the mouth markings onto the snout with straight stitch (see page 141). Add the safety nose using the photo as a guide for positioning and secure with the back. Clip off the surplus nose post.

Adding the fur and mane

Adding the fur on the face can be done in two ways, either with a crochet hook (see page 141) or by threading each strand through with a yarn needle and then tying the ends into a knot close to the fabric. The needle is better for getting into small areas, such as around the eyes.

For the face, cut lengths of A approx. 5in (13cm) long. Starting at the side of the snout, add a line of fur fringe. Add further lines to cover the rest of the marked face area. Brush the yarn to produce the soft fur, then trim to a short length. Cut a few lengths of C and add under the chin, then trim to the length required.

Place one ear piece on top of the other and using A work one round of single crochet through both layers to join. Sew the ear near the top of the head, using the photo as a guide for positioning.

For the mane cut strands of B approx. 7in (18cm) long. Working from the edge of the face outward, add lines of fur fringe, brushing as you go to form the mane.

When the head is complete, spread glue on the front and sides of the cake board. Lay the back of the face onto the board and press in place. Wrap the snout around the front edge of the board, using the photograph as a guide, and glue this to the back of the board. Add pins through the base all around the side of the board to hold everything in place until the glue has dried. When dry remove the pins.

It may be beneficial to lightly spray the mane with hairspray to keep the fur in place (optional).

This pretty little face will bring a smile to anyone's face and brighten any bathroom, making it a great gift to create to resemble a family pet. A quick and easy project for a crocheter of any level.

bathroom tissue cover

SKILL RATING ● ● ●

YARN AND MATERIALS
King Cole Moments DK (100% polyester), light worsted (DK) weight yarn, 98yd (90m) per 1¾oz (50g) ball
  2 balls of Gray shade 3229 (A)

King Cole Yummy (100% polyester), bulky (chunky) weight yarn, 131yd (120m) per 3½oz (100g) ball
  ⅕ ball of Champagne shade 3477 (B)

Small amount of black light worsted (DK) weight yarn (C)

Small amount of toy fiberfill

20mm pink cat safety nose

Pair of 16mm safety eyes

Bow for decoration (optional)

HOOK AND EQUIPMENT
US H-8 (5mm) crochet hook
Yarn needle

FINISHED SIZE
Approx. 7in (18cm) diameter

ABBREVIATIONS
See page 142.

PATTERN NOTE
The Moments DK yarn is worked with two strands of yarn held together throughout.

MAIN COVER
Round 1: Using A, ch5, join with a sl st to form a ring.
Round 2: Ch3 (counts as first dc), 11dc in ring, join with a sl st. *(12 sts)*
Round 3: Ch3, 1dc in same dc, 2dc in each dc to end, join with a sl st. *(24 sts)*
Round 4: Ch3, 2dc in next dc, [1dc in next dc, 2dc in next dc] to end, join with a sl st. *(36 sts)*
Round 5: Ch1, 1sc in next dc, 1sc in each dc to end, join with a sl st.
Round 6: Ch3, 1dc in next sc, 1dc in each sc to end, join with a sl st.
Rounds 7–16: Ch3, 1dc in next dc, 1dc in each dc to end, join with a sl st.
Fasten off.

SNOUT
Round 1: Using B, ch9.
Round 2: 1sc in 2nd ch from hook (missed ch does not count as sc), 1sc in each ch to last ch, 3sc in last ch, working along bottom of chain, 1sc in each ch to end, 1sc in end of row, join with a sl st. *(18 sts)*
Round 3: Ch1 (counts as first sc), 1sc in each of next 6 sc, [2sc in next sc] twice, 1sc in each of next 7 sc, [2sc in next sc] twice, join with a sl st. *(22 sts)*
Rounds 4–7: Ch1, 1sc in next sc, 1sc in each sc to end, join with a sl st.
Sl st to center of snout.
Fasten off, leaving a length of yarn for forming snout.

BASE OF SNOUT
Row 1: Using B, ch4.
Row 2: 1sc in 2nd ch from hook (missed ch does not count as sc), 1sc in each sc to end. *(3 sts)*
Row 3: Ch1 (counts as first sc), 1sc in same sc, 1sc in each sc to end. *(4 sts)*
Row 4: Ch1, 1sc in same sc, 1sc in each sc to end. *(5 sts)*
Fasten off.

EARS

(make 2)

Row 1: Using A, ch2.

Row 2: 1sc in 2nd ch from hook (missed ch does not count as sc). (*1 st*)

Row 3: Ch1 (counts as first sc), 1sc in same sc. (*2 sts*)

Row 4: Ch1, 1sc in same sc, 1sc in next sc. (*3 sts*)

Row 5: Ch1, 1sc in same sc, 1sc in each sc to end. (*4 sts*)

Row 6: Ch1, 1sc in same sc, 1sc in each sc to end. (*5 sts*)

Row 7: Ch1, 1sc in same sc, 1sc in each sc to end. (*6 sts*)

Row 8: Ch1, 1sc in same sc, 1sc in each sc to end. (*7 sts*)

Row 9: Ch1, 1sc in same sc, 1sc in each sc to end. (*8 sts*)

Row 10: Ch1, 1sc in same sc, 1sc in each sc to end. (*9 sts*)

Row 11: Ch1, 1sc in same sc, 1sc in each sc to end. (*10 sts*)

Fasten off.

TO MAKE UP

To form the two puffed parts of the snout, stuff the snout lightly then wind the yarn end around the center and secure firmly at the back with a stitch. Using C, embroider mouth markings onto the snout. Push the post of the safety nose through the crochet above the mouth marking and secure with the back. Sew the snout to the front of the face, using the photo as a guide for positioning. Stuff the base of the snout lightly then sew below the snout.

Add the safety eyes above the snout and secure with the safety backs (see page 141). Clip off the surplus eye posts so that they sit flat. Sew the ears to the top of the head, using the photos as a guide.

Add a bow embellishment (optional).

Place the main cover over a single roll of toilet paper.

CHAPTER 3

bags and accessories

What a stand-out accessory this pretty little clutch bag will be! Make this pattern one of a kind simply by changing the shades of yarn to resemble your own pet. This project could easily be made into a dainty shoulder bag by adding a chain.

clutch bag

SKILL RATING ● ● ○

YARN AND MATERIALS
King Cole Big Value Super Chunky (100% acrylic), super bulky (super chunky) weight yarn, 90yd (81m) per 3½oz (100g) ball
  1 ball of shade 24 Gray (A)

King Cole Big Value Chunky (100% acrylic), bulky (chunky) weight yarn, 167yd (152m) per 3½oz (100g) ball
  1 ball of shade 3640 Silver (B)

Small amount of black bulky (chunky) weight yarn (C)

8in (20cm) zipper

Small amount of toy fiberfill

18mm pink safety nose

Pair of 20mm safety eyes

HOOK AND EQUIPMENT
US H-8 (5mm) and US J-10 (6mm) crochet hooks

Yarn needle

Pins

Sewing needle and thread

Stiff brush or pet brush

Hairspray (optional)

FINISHED SIZE
10 x 7in (25.5 x 18cm)

ABBREVIATIONS
See page 142.

MAIN BAG
Row 1: Using US J-10 (6mm) hook and A, ch22.
Row 2: 1dc in 3rd ch from hook (missed 2 ch do not count as dc), 1dc in each ch to end. (*20 sts*)
Rows 3–16: Ch3 (counts as first dc), 1dc in next dc, 1dc in each dc to end.
Fasten off.

EYE POST COVER
To cover backs of eyes inside bag.
Row 1: Using US J-10 (6mm) hook and A, ch10.
Row 2: 1sc in 2nd ch from hook (missed ch does not count as sc), 1sc in each ch to end. (*9 sts*)
Row 3: Ch1 (counts as first sc), 1sc in next sc, 1sc in each sc to end.
Fasten off.

SNOUT
Round 1: Using US H-8 (5mm) hook and B, ch8.
Round 2: 1sc in 2nd ch from hook (missed ch does not count as sc), 1sc in each ch to last ch, 3sc in last ch, working along bottom of chain, 1sc in each ch to end, 1sc in end of row, join with a sl st. (*16 sts*)
Round 3: Ch1 (counts as first sc), 1sc in each of next 5 sc, [2sc in next sc] twice, 1sc in each of next 6 sc, [2sc in next sc] twice, join with a sl st. (*20 sts*)
Rounds 4–6: Ch1, 1sc in next sc, 1sc in each sc to end, join with a sl st.
Round 7: Ch1, 1sc in each of next 7 sc, [2sc in next sc] twice, 1sc in each of next 8 sc, [2sc in next sc] twice, join with a sl st. (*24 sts*)
Sl st to center of snout.
Fasten off, leaving a length of yarn for forming snout.

BASE OF SNOUT
Row 1: Using US H-8 (5mm) hook and B, ch3.
Row 2: 1sc in 2nd ch from hook (missed ch does not count as sc), 1sc in next ch. (*2 sts*)
Row 3: Ch1 (counts as first sc), 1sc in same sc, 1sc in each sc to end. (*3 sts*)

Row 4: Ch1, 1sc in same sc, 1sc in each sc to end. (4 sts)
Row 5: Ch1, 1sc in same sc, 1sc in each sc to end. (5 sts)
Fasten off.

EAR FRONT AND BACK
(make 4)
Row 1: Using US H-8 (5mm) hook and B, ch2.
Row 2: 1sc in 2nd ch from hook (missed ch does not count as sc). (1 st)
Row 3: Ch1 (counts as first sc), 1sc in same sc, 1sc in each sc to end. (2 sts)
Row 4: Ch1, 1sc in same sc, 1sc in each sc to end. (3 sts)
Row 5: Ch1, 1sc in same sc, 1sc in each sc to end. (4 sts)
Row 6: Ch1, 1sc in same sc, 1sc in each sc to end. (5 sts)

Row 7: Ch1, 1sc in same sc, 1sc in each sc to end. (6 sts)
Row 8: Ch1, 1sc in same sc, 1sc in each sc to end. (7 sts)
Row 9: Ch1, 1sc in same sc, 1sc in each sc to end. (8 sts)
Row 10: Ch1, 1sc in same sc, 1sc in each sc to end. (9 sts)
Row 11: Ch1, 1sc in same sc, 1sc in each sc to end. (10 sts)
Row 12: Ch1, 1sc in next sc, 1sc in each sc to end.
Row 13: Sc2tog, 1sc in each sc to last 2 sc, sc2tog. (8 sts)
Row 14: Ch1, 1sc in next sc, 1sc in each sc to end.
Fasten off.

TO MAKE UP

Bag

Fold the bag in half lengthwise with right sides together and work a single crochet seam (see page 140) down each side to join. Fasten off and turn right side out. Pin the zipper along the inside top edge of the bag, leaving the zipper teeth slightly visible. Using a needle and thread, sew the zipper in place along each side.

Cat face

To form the two puffed parts of the snout, stuff the snout lightly then wind the yarn end around the center and secure firmly at the back with a stitch. Using C, embroider mouth markings onto the snout. Push the post of the safety nose through the crochet above the mouth marking and secure with the back. Sew the snout to the front of the bag. Stuff the base of the snout lightly and sew beneath the snout.

Attach the safety eyes (see page 141) and then clip off the surplus eye posts. Sew the covers over the eye posts on the inside of the bag.

Place two ears with wrong sides together and work a single crochet seam around all sides to join. Repeat with the other two ears. Fasten off, leaving a length of yarn for sewing to the bag. Sew the ears to the top of the bag using the photo as a guide for positioning.

Adding the fur

Adding the fur on the face can be done in two ways, either with a crochet hook (see page 141) or by threading each strand through with a yarn needle and then tying the ends into a knot close to the fabric. The needle is better for getting into small areas, such as around the eyes.

Cut B into 6in (15cm) lengths. Add lines of fur fringing around and under the snout. Continue all around the face and around the ears. Gently unravel each strand and brush gently to give the yarn a fluffy look. Trim any excess fur to produce the shape required.

It may be beneficial to spray the bag front with hairspray to keep the yarn in place (optional).

black-and-white cat purse

This charming purse will turn heads wherever you go, with its fluffy head and soft, long fur that mimics the cheeky look of the popular black-and-white cat. The front of the bag is crocheted in double crochet then covered with brushed yarn, and the snout and ears are worked in single crochet.

YARN AND MATERIALS
King Cole Big Value Super Chunky (100% acrylic), super bulky (super chunky) weight yarn, 90yd (81m) per 3½oz (100g) ball
  3 balls of shade 008 Black (A)
  ¾oz (20g) of shade 1758 White (B)

King Cole Yummy (100% polyester), bulky (chunky) weight yarn, 131yd (120m) per 3½oz (100g) ball
  ¾oz (20g) of shade 3477 Champagne (C)

Pair of 24mm safety eyes

21mm pink safety nose

Toy fiberfill

Pair of bag handles

HOOK AND EQUIPMENT
US I-9 (5.5mm) crochet hook

Yarn needle

Stiff brush or pet brush

Hairspray (optional)

FINISHED SIZE
Approx. 10½ x 10½in (27 x 27cm)

ABBREVIATIONS
See page 142.

SPECIAL ABBREVIATIONS
FPdc (front post double crochet): a double crochet worked by inserting your hook around the post of the next stitch from front to back to front, rather than into the top two loops of a stitch as you normally would

BPdc (back post double crochet): a double crochet worked by inserting your hook around the post of the next stitch from back to front to back, rather than into the top two loops of a stitch as you normally would

PATTERN NOTES
If the bag is not for a child, as an alternative you could clip off the post from the safety nose and glue it into place. For a young child, embroider the eyes and nose instead (see page 141).

The Yummy yarn can fray very easily at either end. It is recommended that the fluff is pulled away from the cotton for the first 2in (5cm). This produces a short length of the cotton that can be sewn into the work to secure into place. To fasten off in this yarn the same procedure is used.

BAG FRONT AND BACK
(make 2)

Row 1: Using A, ch35.

Row 2: 1dc in 3rd ch from hook (missed 2 ch do not count as dc), 1dc in each ch to end. (*33 sts*)

Row 3: Ch3 (counts as first dc), [1FPdc in next dc, 1BPdc in next dc] to last 2 dc, 1FPdc in next dc, 1dc in last dc.

Row 4: Ch3, [1BPdc in next dc, 1FPdc in next dc] to last 2 dc, 1BPdc in next dc, 1dc in last dc.

Rep Rows 3 and 4 until work measures approx. 10in (25.5cm) finishing with a Row 4.

Fasten off.

SNOUT
Round 1: Using C, ch9, 1sc in 2nd ch from hook (missed ch does not count as sc), 1sc in each ch to last ch, 3sc in last ch, working along bottom of chain, 1sc in each ch to end, 1sc in end of row, join with a sl st. (*18 sts*)

Round 2: Ch1 (counts as first sc), 1sc in each of next 6 sc, [2sc in next sc] twice, 1sc in each of next 7 sc, [2sc in next sc] twice, join with a sl st. (*22 sts*)

Rounds 3–7: Ch1, 1sc in next sc, 1sc in each sc to end, join with a sl st.

Fasten off, leaving a length of yarn for forming nose.

BASE OF SNOUT

Row 1: Using C, ch4.
Row 2: 1sc in 2nd ch from hook (missed ch does not count as sc), 1sc in each ch to end. (*3 sts*)
Row 3: Ch1 (counts as first sc), 1sc in same st, 1sc in each sc to end. (*4 sts*)
Row 4: Ch1, 1sc in same st, 1sc in each sc to end. (*5 sts*)
Row 5: Ch1, 1sc in same st, 1sc in each sc to end. (*6 sts*)
Fasten off.

INNER EARS

(make 2)
Row 1: Using C, ch2.
Row 2: 1sc in 2nd ch from hook (missed ch does not count as sc). (*1 st*)
Row 3: Ch1 (counts as first sc), 1sc in same st. (*2 sts*)
Row 4: Ch1, 1sc in same st, 1sc in next sc. (*3 sts*)
Row 5: Ch1, 1sc in same st, 1sc in each sc to end. (*4 sts*)
Row 6: Ch1, 1sc in same st, 1sc in each sc to end. (*5 sts*)
Row 7: Ch1, 1sc in same st, 1sc in each sc to end. (*6 sts*)
Row 8: Ch1, 1sc in same st, 1sc in each sc to end. (*7 sts*)
Fasten off.

OUTER EARS

(make 2)
Row 1: Using A, ch2.
Row 2: 1sc in 2nd ch from hook (missed ch does not count as sc). (*1 st*)
Row 3: Ch1 (counts as first sc), 1sc in same st. (*2 sts*)
Row 4: Ch1, 1sc in same st, 1sc in next sc. (*3 sts*)
Row 5: Ch1, 1sc in same st, 1sc in each sc to end. (*4 sts*)
Row 6: Ch1, 1sc in same st, 1sc in each sc to end. (*5 sts*)
Row 7: Ch1, 1sc in same st, 1sc in each sc to end. (*6 sts*)
Row 8: Ch1, 1sc in same st, 1sc in each sc to end. (*7 sts*)
Fasten off.

EYE POST COVER

To cover backs of eyes inside bag.
Row 1: Using A, ch13.
Row 2: 1sc in 2nd ch from hook (missed ch does not count as sc), 1sc into each ch to end. (*12 sts*)
Rows 3 and 4: Ch1 (counts as first sc), 1sc in each sc to end.
Fasten off.

TO MAKE UP

Place front and back with right sides together. Using A, work a single crochet seam (see page 140) around the sides and bottom, leaving the top edge open. Turn right side out.

To form the two puffed parts of the snout, stuff the snout lightly then wind the yarn end around the center and secure firmly at the back with a stitch. Using A, embroider mouth markings. Push the post of the safety nose through the crochet above the mouth marking and secure with the back. Sew the snout to the bag using the photo as a guide for positioning. Sew the base of the snout below.

Attach the safety eyes (see page 141) and then clip off the surplus eye posts. Sew the cover over the eye posts on the inside of the bag.

Place an inner ear on top of an outer ear and using A work a single crochet seam through both layers to join together. Work a second round of single crochet around the ear, working 2sc in each corner. Repeat for the second ear. Sew the ears on either side of the top front of the bag, using the photo as a guide for positioning.

ADDING THE FUR

Adding the fur on the face can be done in two ways, either with a crochet hook (see page 141) or by threading each strand through with a yarn needle and then tying the ends into a knot close to the fabric. The needle is better for getting into small areas, such as around the eyes.

Face

Cut lengths of A and B approx. 7in (18cm) long. Starting at the top of the snout with lengths of B, add a line of fur fringe approx. 1in (2.5cm) wide as close to the snout as possible. Add two more lines of fur fringe above the snout, making each line slightly wider. Trim to length required. Add further lines of fur fringe until the fur reaches the top of the bag. Brush the yarn with a stiff brush to produce the soft fur effect and trim to the length required—when brushed up the fur should reach the top of the bag.

Switch to A and continue adding lines of fur fringe approx. 2in (5cm) apart until you have completely covered the face. Brush and trim to length required so that all the fur is the same length.

It may be beneficial to spray the front of the bag lightly with hairspray to keep the yarn in place (optional).

Handles

Join the handles by sewing them to the inside of the bag at the top front and top back.

What head-turners this set of his and hers golf club covers will be! These covers are worked in simple single crochet for the head, with the base consisting of double crochet stitches. This is a versatile pattern to enable you to create a variety of golf club covers in different colors that would make great gifts.

his and hers golf club covers

SKILL RATING ● ● ○

YARN AND MATERIALS
Pink cover
King Cole Big Value Chunky (100% acrylic), bulky (chunky) weight yarn, 167yd (152m) per 3½oz (100g) ball
    ¾oz (20g) of shade 827 Pink (A)

King Cole Hedgerow Chunky (100% acrylic), bulky (chunky) weight yarn, 332yd (304m) per 7oz (200g) ball
    ½ ball of shade 5842 Holly Berry (B)

King Cole Yummy (100% polyester), bulky (chunky) weight yarn, 131yd (120m) per 3½oz (100g) ball
    ¾oz (20g) of shade 3477 Champagne (C)

Blue cover
King Cole Big Value Chunky (100% acrylic), bulky (chunky) weight yarn, 167yd (152m) per 3½oz (100g) ball
    ¾oz (20g) of shade 824 Blue (A)
    ⅞oz (25g) shade 553 Red (D)

King Cole Hedgerow Chunky (100% acrylic), bulky (chunky) weight yarn, 332yd (304m) per 7oz (200g) ball
    ½ ball of shade 5841 Thicket (B)

King Cole Yummy (100% polyester), bulky (chunky) weight yarn, 131yd (120m) per 3½oz (100g) ball
    ¾oz (20g) of shade 3477 Champagne (C)

Both covers
Small amount of black yarn (D)

Pair of 8mm safety eyes

16mm pink safety nose

Toy fiberfill

Pompom maker (optional)

Embellishments of your choice

HOOK AND EQUIPMENT
US H-8 (5mm) crochet hook
Yarn needle

FINISHED SIZE
Approx. 9in (23cm) long

ABBREVIATIONS
See page 142.

SPECIAL ABBREVIATIONS
FPdc (front post double crochet): a double crochet worked by inserting your hook around the post of the next stitch from front to back to front, rather than into the top two loops of a stitch as you normally would

BPdc (back post double crochet): a double crochet worked by inserting your hook around the post of the next stitch from back to front to back, rather than into the top two loops of a stitch as you normally would

PATTERN NOTE
The Yummy yarn can fray very easily at either end. It is recommended that the fluff is pulled away from the cotton for the first 2in (5cm). This produces a short length of the cotton that can be sewn into the work to secure into place. To fasten off in this yarn the same procedure is used.

HAT AND HEAD

Round 1: Using A, ch4, join with a sl st to form a ring.
Round 2: Ch1 (counts as first sc), 7sc in ring, join with a sl st. (*8 sts*)
Round 3: Ch1, 1sc in same sc, 2sc in each sc to end, join with a sl st. (*16 sts*)
Round 4: Ch1, 2sc in next sc, [1sc in next sc, 2sc in next sc] to end, join with a sl st. (*24 sts*)
Round 5: Ch1, 1sc in next sc, 2sc in next sc, [1sc in each of next 2 sc, 2sc in next sc] to end, join with a sl st. (*32 sts*)
Round 6: Ch1, 1sc in each of next 2 sc, 2sc in next sc, [1sc in each of next 3 sc, 2sc in next sc] to end, join with a sl st. (*40 sts*)
Round 7: Ch1, 1sc in each of next 3 sc, 2sc in next sc, [1sc in each of next 4 sc, 2sc in next sc] to end, join with a sl st. (*48 sts*)
Round 8: Ch1, 1scBLO in next sc, 1scBLO in each sc to end, join with a sl st.
Rounds 9–13: Ch1, 1sc in next sc, 1sc in each sc to end, join with a sl st.
Round 14: Change to B, ch1, 1scBLO in next sc, 1scBLO in each sc to end, join with a sl st.
Rounds 15–18: Ch1, 1sc in next sc, 1sc in each sc to end, join with a sl st.
Round 19: Ch1, 1sc in each of next 3 sc, sc2tog, [1sc in each of next 4 sc, sc2tog] to end, join with a sl st. (*40 sts*)
Round 20: Ch1, 1sc in each of next 2 sc, sc2tog, [1sc in each of next 3 sc, sc2tog] to end, join with a sl st. (*32 sts*)
Round 21: Ch1, 1sc in next sc, 1sc in each sc to end, join with a sl st.
Round 22: Ch1, 1sc in next sc, sc2tog, [1sc in each of next 2 sc, sc2tog] to end, join with a sl st. (*24 sts*)
Round 23: Ch3 (counts as first dc), 1dc in next st, 1dc in each st to end, join with a sl st.
Rounds 24–32: Ch3, [1FPdc in next dc, 1BPdc in next dc] to last dc, 1FPdc in next dc, join with a sl st.
Fasten off.

Brim of hat

Join A in front loop of center back stitch of Round 14.
Round 1: Ch1, 1sc in next sc, 1sc in each sc to end, join with a sl st. (*48 sts*)
Round 2: Ch3, 2dc in next sc, [1dc in next sc, 2dc in next sc] to end, join with a sl st. (*72 sts*)
Fasten off.

SNOUT

Round 1: Using C, ch5, 1sc in 2nd ch from hook (missed ch does not count as sc), 1sc in each ch to last ch, 3sc in last ch, working along bottom of chain, 1sc in each ch to end, 1sc in end of row, join with a sl st. (*10 sts*)
Round 2: Ch1 (counts as first sc), 1sc in next sc, 1sc in each sc to end, join with a sl st.
Sl st to center of snout.
Fasten off, leaving a length of yarn for forming nose.

BASE OF SNOUT

Row 1: Using C, ch3.
Row 2: 1sc in 2nd ch from hook (missed ch does not count as sc), 1sc in next ch. (*2 sts*)
Row 3: Ch1 (counts as first sc), 1sc in same sc, 1sc in each sc to end. (*3 sts*)
Fasten off.

EARS

(make 2)
Row 1: Using B, ch2.
Row 2: 1sc in 2nd ch from hook (missed ch does not count as sc). (*1 st*)
Row 3: Ch1 (counts as first sc), 1sc in same sc. (*2 sts*)
Row 4: Ch1, 1sc in same sc, 1sc in each sc to end. (*3 sts*)
Row 5: Ch1, 1sc in same sc, 1sc in each sc to end. (*4 sts*)
Row 6: Ch1, 1sc in same sc, 1sc in each sc to end. (*5 sts*)
Fasten off.

COLLAR

Pink version only. Work with two strands of yarn held together.
Row 1: Using two strands of B held together, ch25.
Row 2: 1sc in 2nd ch from hook (missed ch does not count as sc), 1sc in each ch to end. (*24 sts*)
Fasten off.

SCARF

Blue cover only.
Row 1: Using D, ch4.
Row 2: 1sc in 2nd ch from hook (missed ch does not count as sc), 1sc in each ch to end. (*3 sts*)
Row 3: Ch1 (counts as first sc), 1sc in each of next 2 sc.
Rep Row 3 until work measures the desired length.
Fasten off.

TO MAKE UP

To form the two puffed parts of the snout, stuff the snout lightly then wind the yarn end around the center and secure firmly at the back with a stitch. Using D, embroider the mouth markings onto the snout, using the photo as a guide. Push the post of the safety nose through the crochet above the mouth marking and secure with the back. Sew the snout onto the center of the head, using the photo as a guide. Sew the base of snout in position.

Add the eyes above the snout, using the photo as a guide. Sew each ear to the hat in positions required. Sew the collar or scarf to the neck of your cat.

Sew in any yarn ends (see page 139). Add any extra embellishments to decorate the covers.

Blue cover only
Using D and the pompom maker, follow the manufacturer's instructions to make a pompom and sew onto the top of the cover (optional).

Everyone will be envious of this pretty little shoulder bag. This version has a chain handle, but you could easily add a short crochet handle to make it into a purse instead. The front of the bag is worked in double crochet, and covered with brushed yarn, with the snout made in single crochet.

white cat shoulder bag

SKILL RATING ● ● ○

YARN AND MATERIALS
King Cole Big Value Super Chunky (100% acrylic), super bulky (super chunky) weight, 90yd (81m) per 3½oz (100g) ball
   2 balls of shade 1758 White (A)
   1oz (30g) of shade 030 Pink (B)

Pair of 18mm safety eyes

16mm pink safety nose

Toy fiberfill

6in (15cm) purse frame

Length of chain for shoulder strap (optional)

HOOK AND EQUIPMENT
US I-9 (5.5mm) crochet hook

Hairspray (optional)

Yarn needle

Stiff brush or pet brush

FINISHED SIZE
Approx. 6½ x 6½in (16.5 x 16.5cm)

ABBREVIATIONS
See page 142.

SPECIAL ABBREVIATIONS
FPdc (front post double crochet): a double crochet worked by inserting your hook around the post of the next stitch from front to back to front, rather than into the top two loops of a stitch as you normally would

BPdc (back post double crochet): a double crochet worked by inserting your hook around the post of the next stitch from back to front to back, rather than into the top two loops of a stitch as you normally would

BAG FRONT AND BACK
(make 2)
Row 1: Using A, ch25.
Row 2: 1dc in 3rd ch from hook (missed 2 ch do not count as dc), 1dc in each ch to end. (23 sts)
Row 3: Ch3 (counts as first dc), [1FPdc in next dc, 1BPdc in next dc] to last 2 dc, 1FPdc in next dc, 1dc in last dc.
Row 4: Ch3, [1BPdc in next dc, 1FPdc in next dc] to last 2 dc, 1BPdc in next dc, 1dc in last dc.
Rep Rows 3 and 4 until work measures approx. 6in (15cm).
Fasten off.

SNOUT
Round 1: Using A, ch6, 1sc in 2nd ch from hook (missed ch does not count as sc), 1sc in each ch to last ch, 3sc in last ch, working along bottom of chain, 1sc in each ch to end, 1sc in end of row, join with a sl st. (12 sts)
Round 2: Ch1 (counts as first sc), 1sc in each of next 3 sc, [2sc in next sc] twice, 1sc in each of next 4 sc, [2sc in next sc] twice, join with a sl st. (16 sts)
Rounds 3–5: Ch1, 1sc in next sc, 1sc in each sc to end, join with a sl st.
Fasten off, leaving a length of yarn for forming nose.

BASE OF SNOUT
Round 1: Using A, ch4, join with a sl st to form a ring.
Round 2: Ch1 (counts as first sc), 7sc in ring, join with a sl st. (8 sts)
Fasten off.

INNER EARS
(make 2)
Row 1: Using B, ch2.
Row 2: 1sc in 2nd ch from hook (missed ch does not count as sc). (1 st)
Row 3: Ch1 (counts as first sc), 1sc in same st, 1sc in each sc to end. (2 sts)
Row 4: Ch1, 1sc in same st, 1sc in each sc to end. (3 sts)
Row 5: Ch1, 1sc in same st, 1sc in each sc to end. (4 sts)

Row 6: Ch1, 1sc in same st, 1sc in each sc to end. (*5 sts*)
Row 7: Ch1, 1sc in same st, 1sc in each sc to end. (*6 sts*)
Fasten off.

OUTER EARS
(make 2)
Row 1: Using A, ch2.
Row 2: 1sc in 2nd ch from hook (missed ch does not count as sc). (*1 st*)
Row 3: Ch1 (counts as first sc), 1sc in same st, 1sc in each sc to end. (*2 sts*)
Row 4: Ch1, 1sc in same st, 1sc in each sc to end. (*3 sts*)
Row 5: Ch1, 1sc in same st, 1sc in each sc to end. (*4 sts*)

Row 6: Ch1, 1sc in same st, 1sc in each sc to end. (*5 sts*)
Row 7: Ch1, 1sc in same st, 1sc in each sc to end. (*6 sts*)
Fasten off.

EYE POST COVER
To cover backs of eyes inside bag.
Row 1: Using A, ch10.
Row 2: 1sc in 2nd ch from hook (missed ch does not count as sc), 1sc in each ch to end. (*9 sts*)
Rows 3 and 4: Ch1 (counts as first sc), 1 sc in next sc, 1sc in each sc to end.
Fasten off.

TO MAKE UP

Place front and back with right sides together. Using A, work a single crochet seam (see page 140) around the sides and bottom, beginning and ending approx. 1in (2.5cm) down from the top edge at each side. Turn right side out.

To form the two puffed parts of the snout, stuff the snout lightly then wind the yarn end around the center and secure firmly at the back with a stitch. Using B, embroider the mouth markings. Push the post of the safety nose through the crochet above the mouth marking and secure with the back. Sew the snout to the bag using the photo as a guide for positioning. Sew the base of the snout below.

Attach the safety eyes (see page 141) and then clip off the surplus eye posts. Sew the cover over the eye posts on the inside of the bag.

Place an inner ear on top of an outer ear and using A work a single crochet seam through both layers to join together. Repeat for the second ear. Sew the ears on either side of the top front of the bag, using the photo as a guide for positioning.

Sew the purse frame in place.

ADDING THE FUR

Adding the fur on the face can be done in two ways, either with a crochet hook (see page 141) or by threading each strand through with a yarn needle and then tying the ends in a knot close to the fabric. The needle is better for getting into small areas, such as around the eyes.

Cut A into approx. 7in (18cm) lengths. Starting at the side of the nose, add a line of fur fringe all around the face keeping as close to the snout as possible. Continue adding lines of fur fringe approx. 2in (5cm) apart until you have completely covered the face. Brush the yarn with a stiff brush to create the soft fur effect and trim to length required so that all the fur is the same length.

It may be beneficial to spray the front of the bag lightly with hairspray to keep the yarn in place (optional).

Handle/strap

Add a length of chain to the top of the purse clasp to create a handle or strap (optional).

winter scarf

This scarf is just that little bit different. It's crocheted in a self-patterning bulky yarn to give its unique look. Crocheted in single and double crochet stitches throughout, this is an excellent project for all skill levels.

SKILL RATING ● ○ ○

YARN AND MATERIALS
King Cole Safari Chunky (100% acrylic), bulky (chunky) weight yarn, 311yd (285m) per 5¼oz (150g) ball
  4 balls of shade 5000 Elephant (A)

Small amount of black bulky (chunky) weight yarn (B)

Small amount of pink bulky (chunky) weight yarn (C)

Toy fiberfill

Pair of 15mm safety eyes

HOOK AND EQUIPMENT
US H-8 (5mm) crochet hook

FINISHED LENGTH
Adult size 84in (214cm)

ABBREVIATIONS
See page 142.

PATTERN NOTE
If the scarf is to be crocheted for a child, it could be made shorter and the safety eyes could be omitted and embroidered instead (see page 141).

MAIN SCARF

Row 1: Using A, ch54.

Row 2: 1dc in 3rd ch from hook (missed 2 ch do not count as dc), 1dc in each ch to end. (*52 sts*)

Rows 3–90: Ch3 (counts as first dc), 1dc in next dc, 1dc in each dc to end.

Fasten off.

HEAD

Round 1: Using A, ch4, join with a sl st to form a ring.

Round 2: Ch1 (counts as first sc), 7sc in ring, join with a sl st. (*8 sts*)

Round 3: Ch1, 1sc in same sc, 2sc in each sc to end, join with a sl st. (*16 sts*)

Round 4: Ch1, 2sc in next sc, [1sc in next sc, 2sc in next sc] to end, join with a sl st. (*24 sts*)

Round 5: Ch1, 1sc in next sc, 1sc in each sc to end, join with a sl st.

Round 6: Ch1, 1sc in each of next 4 sc, 2sc in next sc, [1sc in each of next 5 sc, 2sc in next sc] to end, join with a sl st. (*28 sts*)

Round 7: Ch1, 1sc in each of next 5 sc, 2sc in next sc, [1sc in each of next 6 sc, 2sc in next sc] to end, join with a sl st. (*32 sts*)

Round 8: Ch1, 1sc in each of next 2 sc, 2sc in next sc, [1sc in each of next 3 sc, 2sc in next sc] to end join with a sl st. (*40 sts*)

Rounds 9–12: Ch1, 1sc in next sc, 1sc in each sc to end, join with a sl st.

Round 13: Ch1, 1sc in each of next 2 sc, sc2tog, [1sc in each of next 3 sc, sc2tog] to end join with a sl st. (*32 sts*)

Round 14: Ch1, 1sc in next sc, sc2tog, [1sc in each of next 2 sc, sc2tog] to end, join with a sl st. (*24 sts*)

Round 15: Ch1, sc2tog, [1sc in next sc, sc2tog] to end, join with a sl st. (*16 sts*)

Round 16: Ch1, 1sc in next sc, 1sc in each sc to end, join with a sl st.

Fasten off, leaving a length of yarn.

LEGS

(make 4)

Round 1: Using A, ch4, join with a sl st to form a ring.

Round 2: Ch3 (counts as first dc), 7dc in ring, join with a sl st. (*8 sts*)

Round 3: Ch3, 2dc in next dc, [1dc in next dc, 2dc in next dc] to end, join with a sl st. (*12 sts*)

Rounds 4–12: Ch3, 1dc in next dc, 1dc in each dc to end, join with a sl st.

Fasten off, leaving a length of yarn.

TAIL

Round 1: Using A, ch4, join with a sl st to form a ring.

Round 2: Ch3 (counts as first dc), 7dc in ring, join with a sl st. (*8 sts*)

Rounds 3–17: Ch3, 1dc in next dc, 1dc in each dc to end, join with a sl st.

Fasten off, leaving a length of yarn.

EARS

(make 4)

Row 1: Using A, ch2.

Row 2: 1sc in 2nd ch from hook (missed ch does not count as sc). (*1 st*)

Row 3: Ch1 (counts as first sc), 1sc in same sc. (*2 sts*)

Row 4: Ch1, 1sc in same sc, 1sc in next sc. (*3 sts*)

Row 5: Ch1, 1sc in same sc, 1sc in each sc to end. (*4 sts*)

Row 6: Ch1, 1sc in same sc, 1sc in each sc to end. (*5 sts*)

Row 7: Ch1, 1sc in same sc, 1sc in each sc to end. (*6 sts*)

Fasten off.

TO MAKE UP

Fold scarf in half widthwise with right sides together and work a single crochet seam (see page 140) along both long edges and along the bottom seam to join. Turn right side out and sew the final ends together.

Sew across the top of each leg. Sew the back legs onto one end of the scarf at each side. Sew the front legs onto the other end of the scarf at each side.

Sew across the end of the tail and then sew the tail in the middle of the end of the scarf between the two back legs.

Stuff the head to give a slightly protruding snout. Attach the safety eyes and secure with the backs (see page 141). Continue to firmly stuff the remainder of the head. Using the yarn end, draw the remaining stitches together to close the opening.

Using B embroider the mouth markings onto the face. Using C, embroider the nose above the mouth markings. Using A, sew whiskers on either side in straight stitch (see page 141).

Place two ears with wrong sides together and work a single crochet seam around all sides to join. Repeat with the other two ears. Sew the ears to the head, using the photo as a guide for positioning.

Sew the head to the front of the scarf between the front legs.

persian cat tote bag

Every cat lover will want to create this stunning, large tote bag. It's crocheted in super bulky yarn for extra stability, and made in single and double crochet stitches throughout. You could create a bag resembling your own feline friend just by altering the shades of yarn. This pattern could easily be made into a pillow by omitting the handles and adding fiberfill.

SKILL RATING ● ● ○

YARN AND MATERIALS
King Cole Big Value Super Chunky (100% acrylic), super bulky (super chunky) weight yarn, 90yd (81m) per 3½oz (100g) ball
  5 balls of shade 1545 Graphite (A)
  1 ball of shade 24 Gray (B)

King Cole Yummy (100% polyester), bulky (chunky) weight yarn, 131yd (120m) per 3½oz (100g) ball
  ⅓ ball of shade 2219 Silver (C)

Small amount of black bulky (chunky) weight yarn (D)

Pair of 26mm safety eyes

21mm pink safety nose

Toy fiberfill

Clear nylon fishing line for whiskers (optional, see pattern note)

HOOK AND EQUIPMENT
US J-10 (6mm) crochet hook

Yarn needle

Stiff brush or pet brush

Hairspray (optional)

FINISHED SIZE
Approx. length including handles 22in (56cm)
Width 14in (35.5cm)

ABBREVIATIONS
See page 142.

PATTERN NOTES
Longer handles could be produced by adding further rows in the pattern on page 80. To add 3D whiskers as shown in the photos, please see page 142. Do not add them if you are giving this project to a young child.

BAG FRONT AND BACK
(make 2)
Row 1: Using A, ch38.
Row 2: 1dc in 3rd ch from hook (missed 2 ch do not count as dc), 1dc in each ch to end. (36 sts)
Rows 3–20: Ch3 (counts as first dc), 1dc in next dc, 1dc in each dc to end.
Fasten off.

SNOUT
Round 1: Using C, ch11.
Round 2: 1sc in 2nd ch from hook (missed ch does not count as sc), 1sc in each ch to last ch, 3sc in last ch, working along bottom of chain, 1sc in each ch to end, 1sc in end of row, join with a sl st. (22 sts)
Round 3: Ch1 (counts as first sc), 1sc in each of next 8 sc, [2sc in next sc] twice, 1sc in each of next 9 sc, [2sc in next sc] twice, join with a sl st. (26 sts)
Rounds 4–6: Ch1, 1sc in next sc, 1sc in each sc to end, join with a sl st.
Sl st to center of snout.
Fasten off, leaving a length of yarn for forming snout.

BASE OF SNOUT
Row 1: Using C, ch4.
Row 2: 1sc in 2nd ch from hook (missed ch does not count as sc), 1sc in each ch to end. (3 sts)
Row 3: Ch1 (counts as first sc), 1sc in same sc, 1sc in each sc to end. (4 sts)
Row 4: Ch1, 1sc in same sc, 1sc in each sc to end. (5 sts)
Row 5: Ch1, 1sc in same sc, 1sc in each sc to end. (6 sts)
Fasten off.

INNER EARS
(make 2)
Row 1: Using B, ch2.
Row 2: 1sc in 2nd ch from hook (missed ch does not count as sc). (1 st)

Row 3: Ch1 (counts as first sc), 1sc in same sc. (*2 sts*)
Row 4: Ch1, 1sc in same sc, 1sc in next sc. (*3 sts*)
Row 5: Ch1, 1sc in same sc, 1sc in each sc to end. (*4 sts*)
Row 6: Ch1, 1sc in same sc, 1sc in each sc to end. (*5 sts*)
Row 7: Ch1, 1sc in same sc, 1sc in each sc to end. (*6 sts*)
Row 8: Ch1, 1sc in same sc, 1sc in each sc to end. (*7 sts*)
Row 9: Ch1, 1sc in same sc, 1sc in each sc to end. (*8 sts*)
Row 10: Ch1, 1sc in same sc, 1sc in each sc to end.
(*9 sts*)
Row 11: Ch1, 1sc in same sc, 1sc in each sc to end.
(*10 sts*)
Row 12: Ch1, 1sc in next sc, 1sc in each sc to end.
Fasten off.

OUTER EARS
(make 2)
Row 1: Using A, ch2.
Row 2: 1sc in 2nd ch from hook (missed ch does not
count as sc). (*1 st*)
Row 3: Ch1 (counts as first sc), 1sc in same sc. (*2 sts*)
Row 4: Ch1, 1sc in same sc, 1sc in next sc. (*3 sts*)
Row 5: Ch1, 1sc in same sc, 1sc in each sc to end.
(*4 sts*)
Row 6: Ch1, 1sc in same sc, 1sc in each sc to end. (*5 sts*)
Row 7: Ch1, 1sc in same sc, 1sc in each sc to end. (*6 sts*)
Row 8: Ch1, 1sc in same sc, 1sc in each sc to end. (*7 sts*)

Row 9: Ch1, 1sc in same sc, 1sc in each sc to end. (*8 sts*)
Row 10: Ch1, 1sc in same sc, 1sc in each sc to end.
(*9 sts*)
Row 11: Ch1, 1sc in same sc, 1sc in each sc to end.
(*10 sts*)
Row 12: Ch1, 1sc in next sc, 1sc in each sc to end.
Fasten off.

EYE POST COVER

To cover backs of eyes inside bag.
Row 1: Using A, ch16.
Row 2: 1sc in 2nd ch from hook (missed ch does not count as sc), 1sc in each ch to end. (*15 sts*)
Rows 3 and 4: Ch1 (counts as first sc), 1sc in each sc to end.
Fasten off.

HANDLES FOR BAG

(make 2)
Row 1: Using A, ch9.
Row 2: 1dc in 3rd ch from hook (missed 2 ch do not count as dc), 1dc in each ch to end. (*7 sts*)
Rows 3–26: Ch3 (counts as first dc), 1dc in next dc, 1dc in each dc to end.
Fasten off.

TO MAKE UP

Place the back and front pieces of the bag with right sides together. Using A, work a single crochet seam (see page 140) around both sides and bottom of the bag. Turn right side out.

Fold a handle in half and work a single crochet seam along the long edge to close. Repeat for the other handle. Sew the ends of the handles on either side of the top opening.

To form the two puffed parts of the snout, stuff the snout lightly then wind the yarn end around the center and secure firmly at the back with a stitch. Using D, embroider mouth markings onto the snout. Push the post of the safety nose through the crochet above the mouth marking and secure with the back. Clip off the excess post then sew the snout to the front of the bag, using the photo as a guide for positioning. Slightly stuff the base of the snout and sew below the snout.

Attach the safety eyes (see page 141) and then clip off the surplus eye posts. Sew the cover over the eye posts on the inside of the bag.

Place an inner ear on top of an outer ear and using A, work a single crochet seam through both layers to join them together. With a stiff brush, gently brush each ear to give them a fluffy look. Sew the ears to the top of the head in the positions required.

Adding fur

Adding the fur on the face can be done in two ways, either with a crochet hook (see page 141) or by threading each strand through with a yarn needle and then tying the ends in a knot close to the fabric.

The needle is better for getting into small areas, such as around the eyes. Strands can be used either with the same shades together or with a strand of each depending on the coloring required.

Cut A and B into approx. 7in (18cm) lengths. Starting at the top of the snout, add a line of fur fringing above the snout approx. 1in (2.5cm) wide. Add a second line approx. 2in (5cm) higher until the top of the bag is covered. Trim to length required.

Add a line of fur fringing all around the snout and then add another round starting just under the first round, so that when brushed the front of the bag is covered by the previous layer. Continue until the whole front of the bag is covered. With a stiff brush gently brush the strands to give them a fluffy look.

It may be beneficial to spray the bag front with hairspray to keep the yarn in place (optional).

This exquisite shawl will be a real head-turner, made with Safari bulky yarn and finished with big cat footprints. Crocheted in single and double crochet stitches throughout, it's an ideal project for a crocheter who has mastered the granny square.

safari shawl

SKILL RATING ● ● ○

YARN AND MATERIALS
King Cole Safari Chunky (100% acrylic),
bulky (chunky) weight yarn, 311yd (285m)
per 5¼oz (150g) ball
   3 balls of Serengeti shade 5004 (A)

King Cole Big Value Chunky (100% acrylic),
bulky (chunky) weight yarn, 167yd (152m)
per 3½oz (100g) ball
   ⅓ ball of Black shade 554 (B)
   ⅓ ball of Silver shade 3640 (C)

HOOK AND EQUIPMENT
US H-8 (5mm) crochet hook

Yarn needle

8in (20cm) wide piece of card stock

FINISHED SIZE
Width 102in (259cm)
Length without fringe 39in (99cm)

ABBREVIATIONS
See page 142.

MAIN SHAWL
Row 1: Using A, ch8.
Row 2: (4dc, ch3, 1tr) in 8th ch from hook (missed 7 ch counts as 1tr and ch3).
Row 3: Ch7 (counts as 1tr and ch3 here and throughout), (4dc, ch3, 1dc) in first 3-ch sp, (4dc, ch3, 1tr) in last 3-ch sp.
Row 4: Ch7, (4dc, ch3, 1dc) in first 3-ch sp, (4dc, ch3, 1dc) in next 3-ch sp, (4dc, ch3, 1tr) in last 3-ch sp.
Row 5: Ch7, (4dc, ch3, 1dc) in first 3-ch sp, [(4dc, ch3, 1dc) in next 3-ch sp] twice, (4dc, ch3, 1tr) in last 3-ch sp.
Row 6: Ch7, (4dc, ch3, 1dc) in first 3-ch sp, [(4dc, ch3, 1dc) in next 3-ch sp] 3 times, (4dc, ch3, 1tr) in last 3-ch sp.
Row 7: Ch7, (4dc, ch3, 1dc) in first 3-ch sp, *(4dc, ch3, 1dc) in next 3-ch sp; rep from * across, (4dc, ch3, 1tr) in last 3-ch sp.
Rep Row 7 until the desired size is reached.
Fasten off.

PAW PRINT
(make 2 or more)
Round 1: Using B, ch4, join with a sl st to form a ring.
Round 2: Ch2 (counts as first hdc), 8hdc in ring, join with a sl st. (*9 sts*)
Round 3: Ch2, 1hdc in same st, 2hdc in each hdc to end, join with a sl st. (*18 sts*)
Join in C.
Round 4: Using C, ch2, 1hdc in same st, 2hdc in each hdc to end, join with a sl st. (*36 sts*)

Round 5: Ch2, (3dc, ch2, sl st) in same st, [miss 2 hdc, (sl st, ch2, 3dc, ch2, sl st) in next st] 3 times (four toe pads), change to B, 1sc in each hdc to end.

Round 6: Using B, working across toe pads only, *1sc in each st around next pad, spike sc (see page 136) between toe pads working into corresponding stitch in Round 3 using photo as a guide; rep from * twice more, 1sc in each st around last pad, sl st in next st. Fasten off.

TO MAKE UP

Wind A evenly around the card stock, trying not to pile it in one area but moving down the length of the cardboard, building a layer of yarn as you wind. Cut the yarn along the bottom edge of the card stock (only) to make the lengths of fringe.

Take four lengths of yarn and fold them in half to form a loop. Starting at one edge of the shawl and working from the wrong side, insert your crochet hook through the scarf in the 3-ch space and pull the loop through, then pull the ends through the loop (see page 141). Pull tightly to secure. Repeat along both shorter edges of the shawl. Trim if required.

Sew the paw prints onto the shawl using the photo as a guide.

makeup bag

This charming little bag would make a perfect gift for any cat lover. Crocheted throughout in the simple single crochet stitch this would also look great as a clutch bag or, with a strap, could transform into a small shoulder bag.

YARN AND MATERIALS
King Cole Velveteen (100% polyester), super bulky (super chunky) weight yarn, 71yd (65m) per 3½oz (100g) ball
  1½ balls of shade 6125 Bunny Tail Gray (A)

King Cole Yummy (100% polyester), bulky (chunky) weight yarn, 131yd (120m) per 3½oz (100g) ball
  Small amount of shade 3477 Champagne (B)

Small amount of black bulky (chunky) weight yarn (C)

21mm pink cat safety nose

Pair of 24mm green safety eyes

10in (25cm) zipper

HOOK AND EQUIPMENT
US I-9 (5.5mm) crochet hook

Stitch marker

Pins

Sewing needle and thread

FINISHED SIZE
10 x 7in (25.5 x 18cm)

ABBREVIATIONS
See page 142.

PATTERN NOTE
It is advisable to use a stitch marker with this pattern.

MAIN BAG
Row 1: Using A, ch25.
Row 2: 1sc in 2nd ch from hook (missed ch does not count as sc), 1sc in each ch to end. (*24 sts*)
Row 3: Ch1 (counts as first sc), 1sc in next sc, 1sc in each sc to end.
Rep Row 3 until work measures approx. 14in (36cm).
Fasten off.

SNOUT
Round 1: Using B, ch11.
Round 2: 1sc in 2nd ch from hook (missed ch does not count as sc), 1sc in each ch to last ch, 3sc in last ch, working along bottom of chain, 1sc in each ch to end, 1sc in end of row, join with a sl st. (*22 sts*)
Round 3: Ch1 (counts as first sc), 1sc in each of next 8 sc, [2sc in next sc] twice, 1sc in each of next 9 sc, [2sc in next sc] twice, join with a sl st. (*26 sts*)
Rounds 4–6: Ch1, 1sc in next sc, 1sc in each sc to end, join with a sl st.
Sl st to center of snout.
Fasten off, leaving a length of yarn for forming snout.

BASE OF SNOUT
Round 1: Using B, ch3.
Round 2: 1sc in 2nd ch from hook (missed ch does not count as sc), 1sc in next ch. (*2 sts*)
Round 3: Ch1 (counts as first sc), 1sc in same sc, 1sc in next sc. (*3 sts*)
Round 4: Ch1, 1sc in same sc, 1sc in each sc to end. (*4 sts*)
Round 5: Ch1, 1sc in same sc, 1sc in each sc to end. (*5 sts*)
Fasten off.

EARS

(make 2)

Row 1: Using A, ch2.

Row 2: 1sc in 2nd ch from hook (missed ch does not count as sc). (*1 st*)

Row 3: Ch1 (counts as first sc), 1sc in same sc. (*2 sts*)

Row 4: Ch1, 1sc in same sc, 1sc in next sc. (*3 sts*)

Row 5: Ch1, 1sc in same sc, 1sc in each sc to end. (*4 sts*)

Row 6: Ch1, 1sc in same sc, 1sc in each sc to end. (*5 sts*)

Row 7: Ch1, 1sc in same sc, 1sc in each sc to end. (*6 sts*)

Fasten off.

EYE POST COVER

To cover backs of eyes inside bag.

Row 1: Using A, ch16.

Row 2: 1sc in 2nd ch from hook (missed ch does not count as sc), 1sc in each ch to end. (*15 sts*)

Rows 3 and 4: Ch1 (counts as first sc), 1sc in next sc, 1sc in each sc to end.

Fasten off.

TO MAKE UP

Fold main bag in half with right sides together and sew up either side. Turn right side out.

To form the two puffed parts of the snout, stuff the snout lightly then wind the yarn end around the center and secure firmly at the back with a stitch. Using C, embroider mouth markings onto the snout. Push the post of the safety nose through the crochet above the mouth marking and secure with the back, then clip off the surplus post. Sew the snout to the front of the bag, using the photo as a guide for positioning. Stuff the base of the snout lightly and sew beneath the snout. Using C, embroider whiskers in straight stitch (see page 141) on either side of the snout.

Attach the safety eyes (see page 141) and then clip off the surplus eye posts. Sew the cover over the eye posts on the inside of the bag.

Pin the zipper in place along the top edges of the bag, then sew in place with a needle and thread. Sew the ears to the top of the bag using the photo as a guide for positioning.

fluffy cat mug cozies

Be the envy of all your friends when you serve them coffee in these cheeky cat mug cozies. Crocheted in the simple single crochet stitch throughout, they would brighten any table and make perfect gifts to create for any cat lover.

YARN AND MATERIALS
Ginger cat
King Cole Moments
DK (100% polyester),
light worsted (DK) weight
yarn, 98yd (90m) per
1¾oz (50g) ball
   1 ball of Ginger shade
   1876 (A)

King Cole Yummy (100%
polyester), bulky (chunky)
weight yarn, 131yd (120m)
per 3½oz (100g) ball
   1⅛ ball of Champagne
   shade 3477 (B)

Black and white cat
King Cole Moments DK
(100% polyester), light
worsted (DK) weight
yarn, 98yd (90m) per
1¾oz (50g) ball
   1 ball of Black shade
   474 (A)
   1 ball of White shade
   470 (B)

Each cat
Small amount of black
light worsted (DK)
weight yarn (C)

Small amount of toy fiberfill

15mm pink cat safety nose

Pair of 18mm safety eyes

HOOK AND EQUIPMENT
US H-8 (5mm) crochet hook

Yarn needle

FINISHED SIZE
Approx. 4in (10cm)
diameter to fit a standard
ceramic mug

ABBREVIATIONS
See page 142.

PATTERN NOTE
The Moments DK yarn
is worked with two
strands held together
for this pattern.

MUG COZY
Row 1: Using A, ch33.
Row 2: 1sc in 2nd ch from hook (missed ch does
not count as sc), 1sc in each ch to end. (*32 sts*)
Rows 3–14: Ch1 (counts as first sc), 1sc in next sc,
1sc in each sc to end.
Fasten off.

EYE POST COVER
To cover backs of eyes inside cozy.
Row 1: Using A, ch8.
Row 2: 1sc in 2nd ch from hook (missed ch does
not count as sc), 1sc in each ch to end. (*7 sts*)
Row 3: Ch1 (counts as first sc), 1sc in next sc,
1sc in each sc to end.
Fasten off, leaving a length of yarn for sewing
to inside of cozy.

SNOUT
Round 1: Using B, ch6.
Round 2: 1sc in 2nd ch from hook (missed ch does not
count as sc), 1sc in each ch to last ch, 3sc in last ch,
working along bottom of chain, 1sc in each ch to end,
1sc in end of row, join with a sl st. (*12 sts*)
Round 3: Ch1 (counts as first sc), 1sc in each of next
4 sc, 2sc in next sc, 1sc in each of next 5sc, 2sc
in last sc, join with a sl st. (*14 sts*)

Rounds 4-6: Ch1, 1sc in next sc, 1sc in each sc to end, join with a sl st.
Sl st to center of snout.
Fasten off, leaving a length of yarn for forming snout.

BASE OF SNOUT
Round 1: Using B, ch4, join with a sl st to form a ring.
Round 2: Ch1 (counts as first sc), 9sc in ring, join with a sl st. (*10 sts*)
Fasten off.

STRIPE ABOVE SNOUT
Black and white cat only.
Row 1: Using B, ch8.
Row 2: 1sc in 2nd ch from hook (missed ch does not count as sc), 1sc in each ch to end. (*7 sts*)
Fasten off.

EARS
(make 2)
Row 1: Using A, ch2.
Row 2: 1sc in 2nd ch from hook (missed ch does not count as sc). (*1 st*)
Row 3: Ch1 (counts as first sc), 1sc in same sc. (*2 sts*)
Row 4: Ch1, 1sc in same sc, 1sc in each sc to end. (*3 sts*)
Row 5: Ch1, 1sc in same sc, 1sc in each sc to end. (*4 sts*)
Row 6: Ch1, 1sc in same sc, 1sc in each sc to end. (*5 sts*)
Row 7: Ch1, 1sc in same sc, 1sc in each sc to end. (*6 sts*)
Fasten off.

TO MAKE UP
Fold the mug cozy in half, widthways with wrong sides together. Sew a seam (see page 139) for approx. ½in (1cm) at top and bottom, leaving a large gap for the mug handle.

Stuff the snout lightly and then wind the yarn end tightly around the center to form two puffed parts. Secure firmly at the back with a stitch. Using C in a yarn needle, sew the mouth markings. Push the post of the safety nose through the crochet above the mouth markings and secure with the back. Sew the snout to the center of the mug cozy. Stuff the base of the snout lightly then sew below the snout.

Attach the safety eyes (see page 141) and then clip off the surplus eye posts. Sew the cover over the eye posts on the inside of the cozy. Sew the ears to the cozy, using the photos as a guide for positioning.

On the black and white cat only, sew the stripe above the snout.

Fit the cozy onto the mug.

Be the envy of all your craft buddies with these quick and simple crocheted tape measure covers. They are easy to create in simple single crochet throughout, making them great gifts to crochet for friends and cat lovers alike.

tape measure covers

SKILL RATING ● ○ ○

YARN AND MATERIALS
White cat
King Cole Moments DK (100% polyester), light worsted (DK) weight yarn, 98yd (90m) per 1¾oz (50g) ball
½ ball of White shade 470 (A)

Ginger cat
King Cole Moments DK (100% polyester) light worsted (DK) weight yarn, 98yd (90m) per 1¾oz (50g) ball
½ ball of Ginger shade 1876 (A)

Both cats
King Cole Truffle Glitz (91% polyamide, 9% glitter), light worsted (DK) weight yarn, 170yd (156m) per 3½oz (100g) ball
Small amount of Snow White shade 5420 (B)

Small amount of pink light worsted (DK) weight yarn (C)

Pair of 12mm green cat safety eyes

2½in (6cm) round tape measure

Bow embellishment for decoration (optional)

HOOK AND EQUIPMENT
US G-6 (4mm) crochet hook

Yarn needle

FINISHED SIZE
3 x 3½in (7.5 x 9cm)

ABBREVIATIONS
See page 142.

PATTERN NOTE
The Moments and Truffle Glitz DK yarns are both worked with two strands of yarn held together throughout.

FRONT OF COVER
Round 1: Using A, ch4, join with a sl st to form a ring.
Round 2: Ch1 (counts as first sc), 7sc in ring, join with a sl st. (*8 sts*)
Round 3: Ch1, 1sc in same sc, 2sc in each sc to end, join with a sl st. (*16 sts*)
Round 4: Ch1, 2sc in next sc, [1sc in next sc, 2sc in next sc] to end, join with a sl st. (*24 sts*)
Round 5: Ch1, 1scBLO in next sc, 1scBLO in each sc to end, join with a sl st.
Fasten off.

BACK OF COVER
Work as Rounds 1–4 of Front of Cover.
Fasten off.

SNOUT
Round 1: Using B, ch4.
Round 2: 1sc in 2nd ch from hook (missed ch does not count as sc), 1sc in each ch to last ch, 2sc in last ch, working along bottom of chain, 1sc in each ch to end, join with a sl st. (*6 sts*)
Fasten off.

EARS
(make 2)
Row 1: Using A, ch2.
Row 2: 1sc in 2nd ch from hook (missed ch does not count as sc). (*1 st*)
Row 3: Ch1 (counts as first sc), 1sc in same sc. (*2 sts*)
Row 4: Ch1, 1sc in same sc, 1sc in next sc. (*3 sts*)
Row 5: Ch1, 1sc in same sc, 1sc in each sc to end. (*4 sts*)
Row 6: Ch1, 1sc in same sc, 1sc in each sc to end. (*5 sts*)
Fasten off.

TO MAKE UP

Sew the snout onto the front of the cover, using the photo as a guide for positioning. Using C, embroider the nose markings. Attach the safety eyes (see page 141) and then clip off the surplus eye posts so they lie flat.

Sew the back of the cover to the front with wrong sides together, leaving a gap of approx. 2in (5cm). Insert the tape measure through the gap, ensuring that the end with the tab is showing at the bottom of the gap. Sew the gap closed leaving a small opening for the end of the tape measure.

Sew the ears on either side at the top of the head.
Add any embellishments (optional).

This unusual little pajama case for children is sure to be a firm favorite. It is crocheted in very soft yarn in single crochet stitch throughout. Perfect for sitting on a bed, this case also doubles up as a cuddly toy and will be admired by all who see it.

child's pajama case

SKILL RATING ● ◦ ◦

YARN AND MATERIALS
King Cole Yummy (100% polyester), bulky (chunky) weight yarn, 87yd (80m) per 3½oz (100g) ball
  2 balls of Sherbert Rose shade 4744 (A)

King Cole Yummy (100% polyester), bulky (chunky) weight yarn, 131yd (120m) per 3½oz (100g) ball
  ⅛ balls of Mint shade 2221 (B)

Small amount of pink light worsted (DK) yarn (C)

Small amount of black light worsted (DK) yarn (D)

Small amount of toy fiberfill

Pair of 24mm cat safety eyes

8in (20cm) zipper

HOOK AND EQUIPMENT
US H-8 (5mm) crochet hook

Yarn needle

Pins

Sewing needle and thread

FINISHED SIZE
Width 12in (30cm)
Height 14in (35.5cm)

ABBREVIATIONS
See page 142.

PATTERN NOTE
If this is to be made for young children, embroider the eyes (see page 141) instead of using the safety eyes stated in the pattern.

CASE FRONT
Round 1: Using A, ch4, join with a sl st to form a ring.
Round 2: Ch1 (counts as first sc), 7sc in ring, join with a sl st. (*8 sts*)
Round 3: Ch1, 1sc in same sc, 2sc in each sc to end, join with a sl st. (*16 sts*)
Round 4: Ch1, 2sc in next sc, [1sc in next sc, 2sc in next sc] to end, join with a sl st. (*24 sts*)
Round 5: Ch1, 1sc in next sc, 2sc in next sc, [1sc in each of next 2 sc, 2sc in next sc] to end, join with a sl st. (*32 sts*)
Round 7: Ch1, 1sc in each of next 2 sc, 2sc in next sc, [1sc in each of next 3 sc, 2sc in next sc] to end, join with a sl st. (*40 sts*)
Round 8: Ch1, 1sc in each of next 3 sc, 2sc in next sc, [1sc in each of next 4 sc, 2sc in next sc] to end, join with a sl st. (*48 sts*)
Round 9: Ch1, 1sc in each of next 4 sc, 2sc in next sc, [1sc in each of next 5 sc, 2sc in next sc] to end, join with a sl st. (*56 sts*)
Round 10: Ch1, 1sc in each of next 5 sc, 2sc in next sc, [1sc in each of next 6 sc, 2sc in next sc] to end, join with a sl st. (*64 sts*)
Round 11: Ch1, 1sc in each of next 6 sc, 2sc in next sc, [1sc in each of next 7 sc, 2sc in next sc] to end, join with a sl st. (*72 sts*)
Round 12: Ch1, 1sc in each of next 7 sc, 2sc in next sc, [1sc in each of next 8 sc, 2sc in next sc] to end, join with a sl st. (*80 sts*)
Round 13: Ch1, 1sc in each of next 8 sc, 2sc in next sc, [1sc in each of next 9 sc, 2sc in next sc] to end, join with a sl st. (*88 sts*)
Round 14: Ch1, 1sc in next sc, 1sc in each sc to end, join with a sl st.
Round 15: Ch1, 1scBLO in next sc, 1scBLO in each sc to end, join with a sl st.
Rounds 16 and 17: Ch1, 1sc in next sc, 1sc in each sc to end, join with a sl st.
Fasten off.

CASE BACK
Work as for front to end of Round 15.
Fasten off.

SNOUT

Round 1: Using B, ch6.
Round 2: 1sc in 2nd ch from hook (missed ch does not count as sc), 1sc in each ch to last ch, 3sc in last ch, working along bottom of chain, 1sc in each ch to end, 1sc in end of row, join with a sl st. (*12 sts*)

Round 3: Ch1 (counts as first sc), 1sc in each of next 4 sc, [2sc in next sc] twice, 1sc in each sc to last 2 sc, [2sc in next sc] twice, join with a sl st. (*16 sts*)
Round 4: Ch1, 1sc in each of next 7 sc, 2sc in next sc, 1sc in each sc to last sc, 2sc in last sc, join with a sl st. (*18 sts*)
Fasten off.

INNER EARS

(make 2)

Row 1: Using B, ch2.

Row 2: 1sc in 2nd ch from hook (missed ch does not count as sc). (*1 st*)

Row 3: Ch1 (counts as first sc), 1sc in same sc. (*2 sts*)

Row 4: Ch1, 1sc in same sc, 1sc in next sc to end. (*3 sts*)

Row 5: Ch1, 1sc in same sc, 1sc in each sc to end. (*4 sts*)

Row 6: Ch1, 1sc in same sc, 1sc in each sc to end. (*5 sts*)

Row 7: Ch1, 1sc in same sc, 1sc in each sc to end. (*6 sts*)

Row 8: Ch1, 1sc in same sc, 1sc in each sc to end. (*7 sts*)

Row 9: Ch1, 1sc in same sc, 1sc in each sc to end. (*8 sts*)

Row 10: Ch1, 1sc in same sc, 1sc in each sc to end. (*9 sts*)

Row 11: Ch1, 1sc in same sc, 1sc in each sc to end. (*10 sts*)

Fasten off.

OUTER EARS

(make 2)

Row 1: Using A, ch2.

Row 2: 1sc in 2nd ch from hook (missed ch does not count as sc). (*1 st*)

Row 3: Ch1 (counts as first sc), 1sc in same sc. (*2 sts*)

Row 4: Ch1, 1sc in same sc, 1sc in each sc to end. (*3 sts*)

Row 5: Ch1, 1sc in same sc, 1sc in each sc to end. (*4 sts*)

Row 6: Ch1, 1sc in same sc, 1sc in each sc to end. (*5 sts*)

Row 7: Ch1, 1sc in same sc, 1sc in each sc to end. (*6 sts*)

Row 8: Ch1, 1sc in same sc, 1sc in each sc to end. (*7 sts*)

Fasten off.

TO MAKE UP

Pin front and back of case together with right sides together, leaving a gap of approx. 8in (20cm) across the center of the top of the head. Work single crochet through both layers to join, leaving the top open. Turn right side out.

Using C, embroider the nose in satin stitch (see page 141) on the snout. Using D, embroider the mouth markings and whiskers in straight stitch (see page 141), using the photo as a guide. Sew the snout to the front of the head, adding a little stuffing as you go.

Attach the safety eyes (see page 141) and then clip off the surplus eye posts. Using A, oversew over the eye posts on the inside of the cover. Using D, sew an eyebrow curve over each eye in a series of straight stitches.

Place an inner ear on top of an outer ear and using A work a single crochet seam (see page 140) through both layers to join. Sew the ears to the top of the head, using the photo as a guide.

Open and pin the zipper tapes in place along each side of the top opening. Sew the zipper in place with a sewing needle and thread.

child's slipper socks

Crochet some soft and snuggly slipper socks as gifts for children. With a pretty little cat motif added to give the socks extra charm, this is a simple pattern that would be perfect for those wanting to learn to crochet.

YARN AND MATERIALS

Small
King Cole Yummy (100% polyester),
bulky (chunky) weight yarn, 131yd (120m)
per 3½oz (100g) ball
 1 ball of Cappuccino shade 2210 (A)
 ⅛ ball of Teddy shade 3404 (B)

Large
King Cole Yummy (100% polyester),
bulky (chunky) weight yarn, 131yd (120m)
per 3½oz (100g) ball
 1 ball of Latte shade 3225 (A)
 ⅛ ball of Silver shade 2219 (B)

Both sizes
Small amount of black light
worsted (DK) yarn (C)

2 pairs of 12mm cat safety eyes

Pair of 14mm pink cat safety noses

Bow embellishments for decoration
(optional)

HOOK AND EQUIPMENT

Small: US H-8 (5mm) crochet hook

Large: US J-10 (6mm) crochet hook

Yarn needle

Sewing needle and thread (optional)

FINISHED SIZE

Note: Foot length is adjustable.
Small approx. 8¼in (21cm) foot
circumference, 8in (20cm) foot length
Large approx. 11in (28cm) foot
circumference, 9in (22.5cm) foot length

ABBREVIATIONS

See page 142.

PATTERN NOTE

If these slippers are to be made for young
children, embroider the eyes and nose (see
page 141) instead of using the safety eyes
and nose stated in the pattern.

LARGE SLIPPER SOCKS

(make 2)
Foot
Round 1: Using US J-10 (6mm) hook and A, ch5, join with a sl st to
form a ring.
Round 2: Ch3 (counts as first dc), 9dc in ring, join with a sl st. (*10 sts*)
Round 3: Ch3, 1dc in same dc, 2dc in each dc to end, join with a sl st.
(*20 sts*)
Rounds 4–7: Ch3, 1dc in next dc, 1dc in each dc to end, join with
a sl st.
Note: More or fewer rounds may be worked here to lengthen or
shorten the foot, before continuing to Round 8.
Round 8: Ch3, 1dc in each of the next 14 dc, 1hdc in next dc, 1sc in
each of next 3 dc, 1hdc in last dc, join with a sl st.
Round 9: Ch3, 1dc in each of next 14 dc, turn, leaving rem 5 sts
unworked. (*15 sts*)
Rounds 10 and 11: Ch3, 1dc in next dc, 1dc in each dc to end, turn.
Round 12: Ch3, 1dc in each of next 5 dc, dc3tog, 1dc in each of
next 6 dc. (*13 sts*)
Do not fasten off.
Sl st in top of first st of this row to create heel.
Turn slipper so toe is facing away from you.

Leg

Begin to work up ankle.

Round 1: Ch1 (counts as first sc), work sc evenly around ankle opening, working 2sc in each row end and 1sc in each st along front of foot, join with a sl st.

Round 2: Ch3 (counts as first dc), 1dc in next sc, 1dc in each sc to end, join with a sl st.

Round 3: Ch3, 1dc in next dc, 1dc in each dc to end, join with a sl st.

Rep Round 3 until desired leg length is reached.

Fasten off.

SMALL SLIPPER SOCKS

Make as for large size using US H-8 (5mm) hook.

CAT MOTIF

(make 2 for each pair of socks)

Round 1: Using B, ch5, join with a sl st to form a ring.

Round 2: Ch3 (counts as first dc), 9dc in ring, join with a sl st. (*10 sts*)

Round 3: Ch3, 1dc in same dc, 2dc in each dc to end, join with a sl st. (*20 sts*)

Fasten off.

CAT EARS

(make 4 for each pair of socks)

Row 1: Using B, ch2.

Row 2: 1sc in 2nd ch from hook (missed ch does not count as sc). (*1 st*)

Row 3: Ch1 (counts as first sc), 1sc in same sc. (*2 sts*)

Row 4: Ch1, 1sc in same sc, 1sc in next sc. (*3 sts*)

Row 5: Ch1, 1sc in same sc, 1sc in each sc to end. (*4 sts*)

Fasten off.

TO MAKE UP

Turn the sock inside out and sew up the heel seam (see page 139), then turn right side out.

Fold over the last round at the top of the leg for a cuff, if required, and secure with a couple of stitches.

Cat head motifs

Sew the ears to the top of the head using the photo as a guide.

Insert the safety eyes and nose (see page 141) and secure with the safety backs. Clip off the surplus eye and nose posts.

Using C, embroider the mouth markings to each motif, using the photograph as a guide.

Sew a head to each slipper.

Add any embellishments.

CHAPTER 4

decorative and cuddly cats

Who wouldn't want this pretty cuddly cat as a companion? Crocheted in the luxuriously soft Velveteen yarn in single crochet, Kathryn will look great on a couch or would be a perfect gift for any cat lover. If Kathryn is to be given to a child, omit the safety eyes and nose and embroider these onto the face instead.

kathryn the cuddly cat

SKILL RATING ● ● ●

YARN AND MATERIALS
King Cole Velveteen (100% polyester), super bulky (super chunky) weight yarn, 71yd (65m) per 3½oz (100g) ball
    2 balls of Shade 6123 Shadowy Ash (A)

King Cole Cottagespun Chunky (100% acrylic), bulky (chunky) weight yarn, 246yd (225m) per 5¼oz (150g) ball
    1 ball of shade 6000 Winterberry Red (B)

King Cole Big Value Super Chunky (100% acrylic), super bulky (super chunky) weight yarn, 90yd (81m) per 3½oz (100g) ball
    ¾oz (20g) of shade 024 Gray (C)

King Cole Super Yummy (100% polyester), super bulky (super chunky) weight yarn, 44yd (40m) per 3½oz (100g) ball
    ¾oz (20g) of shade 4874
    Ice White (D, optional)

Small amount of bulky (chunky) weight yarn in pink (E)

Pair of 20mm safety eyes

20mm pink safety nose

Toy fiberfill

Embellishments of your choice

HOOK AND EQUIPMENT
US H-8 (5mm) crochet hook

Stitch marker

Yarn needle

FINISHED SIZE
Standing height approx. 22in (56cm)

ABBREVIATIONS
See page 142.

PATTERN NOTES
It is advisable to use a stitch marker with the Velveteen yarn.
If giving the cat to a young child, substitute the embellisments and the safety eyes and nose with embroidery in yarn (see page 141).
The Super Yummy yarn can fray very easily at either end. It is recommended that the fluff is pulled away from the cotton for the first 2in (5cm). This produces a short length of the cotton that can be sewn into the work to secure into place. To fasten off in this yarn the same procedure is used.

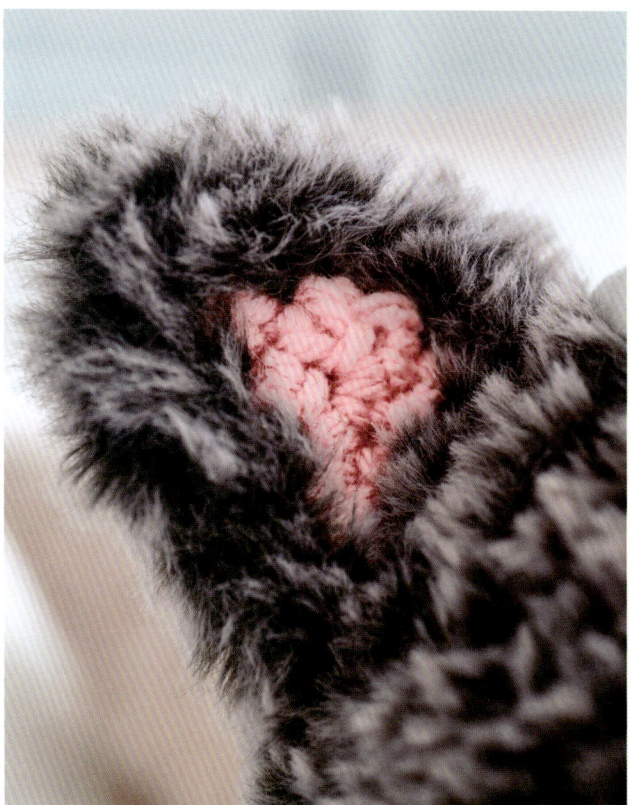

BODY

Round 1: Using A, ch5, join with a sl st to form a ring.

Round 2: Ch1 (counts as first sc), 11sc in ring, join with a sl st. (*12 sts*)

Round 3: Ch1, 1sc in same sc, 2sc in each sc to end, join with a sl st. (*24 sts*)

Round 4: Ch1, 1sc in each of next 7 sc, [2sc in next sc] 4 times, 1sc in each of next 8 sc, [2sc in next sc] 4 times, join with a sl st. (*32 sts*)

Round 5: Ch1, 1sc in next sc, 1sc in each sc to end, join with a sl st.

Round 6: Ch1, 1sc in each of next 2 sc, 2sc in next sc, [1sc in each of next 3 sc, 2sc in next sc] to end, join with a sl st. (*40 sts*)

Round 7: Ch1, 1sc in next sc, 1sc in each sc to end, join with a sl st.

Round 8: Ch1, 1sc in each of next 3 sc, 2sc in next sc, [1sc in each of next 4 sc, 2sc in next sc] to end, join with a sl st. (48 sts)

Rounds 9–20: Ch1, 1sc in next sc, 1sc in each sc to end, join with a sl st.

Round 21: Change to B, ch1, 1sc in next sc, 1sc in each sc to end, join with a sl st.

Round 22: Ch1, 1scBLO in next sc, 1scBLO in each sc to end, join with a sl st.

Rounds 23–27: Ch1, 1sc in next sc, 1sc in each sc to end, join with a sl st.

Round 28: Ch1, 1sc in each of next 3 sc, sc2tog, [1sc in each of next 4 sc, sc2tog] to end, join with a sl st. (*40 sts*)

Rounds 29 and 30: Ch1, 1sc in next sc, 1sc in each sc to end, join with a sl st.

Round 31: Ch1, 1sc in each of next 2 sc, sc2tog, [1sc in each of next 3 sc, sc2tog] to end, join with a sl st. (*32 sts*)

Rounds 32 and 33: Ch1, 1sc in next sc, 1sc in each sc to end, join with a sl st.

Round 34: Ch1, 1sc in each of next 7 sc, [sc2tog] 4 times, 1c in each of next 8 sc, [sc2tog] 4 times, join with a sl st. (*24 sts*)

Rounds 35 and 36: Ch1, 1sc in next sc, 1sc in each sc to end, join with a sl st.

Turn so that wrong side is on outside. Stuff body firmly.

Round 37: [Sc2tog] to end, join with a sl st. (*12 sts*)
Fasten off, leaving a length of yarn.
Thread yarn end onto needle, gather remaining sts together, fasten off.

HEAD

Round 1: Using A, ch5, join with a sl st to form a ring.
Round 2: Ch1 (counts as first sc), 11sc in ring, join with a sl st. (*12 sts*)
Round 3: Ch1, 1sc in same sc, 2sc in each sc to end, join with a sl st. (*24 sts*)
Round 4: Ch1, 1sc in each of next 7 sc, [2sc in next sc] 4 times, 1sc in each of next 8 sc, [2sc in next sc] 4 times, join with a sl st. (*32 sts*)
Round 5: Ch1, 1sc in next sc, 1sc in each sc to end, join with a sl st.
Round 6: Ch1, 1sc in each of next 2 sc, 2sc in next sc, [1sc in each of next 3 sc, 2sc in next sc] to end, join with a sl st. (*40 sts*)
Rounds 7–10: Ch1, 1sc in next sc, 1sc in each sc to end, join with a sl st.
Round 11: Ch1, 1sc in next sc, sc2tog, [1sc in each of next 2 sc, sc2tog] to end, join with a sl st. (*30 sts*)
Round 12: Ch1, sc2tog, [1sc in next sc, sc2tog] to end, join with a sl st. (*20 sts*)
Round 13: Ch1, 1sc in next sc, 1sc in each sc to end, join with a sl st.
Fasten off.

SNOUT

Round 1: Using C, ch8, 1sc in 2nd ch from hook (missed ch does not count as sc), 1sc in each ch to last ch, 3sc in last ch, working along bottom of chain, 1sc in each ch to end, 1sc in end of row, join with a sl st. (*16 sts*)
Round 2: Ch1 (counts as first sc), 1sc in each of next 5 sc, [2sc in next sc] twice, 1sc in each of next 6 sc, [2sc in next sc] twice, join with a sl st. (*20 sts*)
Rounds 3–5: Ch1, 1sc in next sc, 1sc in each sc to end, join with a sl st.
Fasten off, leaving a length of yarn for forming nose.

BASE OF SNOUT

Row 1: Using C, ch3.
Row 2: 1sc in 2nd ch from hook (missed ch does not count as sc), 1sc in next ch. (*2 sts*)
Row 3: Ch1 (counts as first sc), 1sc in same sc, 1sc in each sc to end. (*3 sts*)
Row 4: Ch1, 1sc in same sc, 1sc in each sc to end. (*4 sts*)
Fasten off.

INNER EAR

Row 1: Using E, ch2.
Row 2: 1sc in 2nd ch from hook (missed ch does not count as sc). (*1 st*)
Row 3: Ch1 (counts as first sc), 1sc in same sc. (*2 sts*)
Row 4: Ch1, 1sc in same sc, 1sc in each sc to end. (*3 sts*)
Row 5: Ch1, 1sc in same sc, 1sc in each sc to end. (*4 sts*)
Row 6: Ch1, 1sc in same sc, 1sc in each sc to end. (*5 sts*)
Fasten off.

OUTER EAR

Row 1: Using A, ch2.
Row 2: 1sc in 2nd ch from hook (missed ch does not count as sc). (*1 st*)
Row 3: Ch1 (counts as first sc), 1sc in same sc. (*2 sts*)
Row 4: Ch1, 1sc in same sc, 1sc in each sc to end. (*3 sts*)
Row 5: Ch1, 1sc in same sc, 1sc in each sc to end. (*4 sts*)
Row 6: Ch1, 1sc in same sc, 1sc in each sc to end. (*5 sts*)
Fasten off.

ARMS

(make 2)

Round 1: Using A, ch4, join with a sl st to form a ring.

Round 2: Ch1 (counts as first sc), 7sc in ring, join with a sl st. (*8 sts*)

Round 3: Ch1, 2sc in next sc, [1sc in next sc, 2sc in next sc] to end, join with a sl st. (*12 sts*)

Round 4: Ch1, 1sc in next sc, 1sc in each sc to end, join with a sl st.

Round 5: Ch1, 1sc in next sc, 2sc in next sc, [1sc in each of next 2 sc, 2sc in next sc] to end, join with a sl st. (*16 sts*)

Round 6: Ch1, 1sc in next sc, 1sc in each sc to end, join with a sl st.

Rounds 7 and 8: Change to B, ch1, 1sc in next sc, 1sc in each sc to end, join with a sl st.

Round 9: Ch1, 1sc in next sc, sc2tog, [1sc in each of next 2 sc, sc2tog] to end, join with a sl st. (*12 sts*)

Rounds 10–20: Ch1, 1sc in next sc, 1sc in each sc to end, join with a sl st.

Fasten off.

LEGS

(make 2)

Round 1: Using B, ch4, join with a sl st to form a ring.

Round 2: Ch1 (counts as first sc), 7sc in ring, join with a sl st. (*8 sts*)

Round 3: Ch1, 2sc in next sc, [1sc in next sc, 2sc in next sc] to end, join with a sl st. (*12 sts*)

Round 4: Ch1, 1sc in next sc, 2sc in next sc, [1sc in each of next 2 sc, 2sc in next sc] to end, join with a sl st. (*16 sts*)

Round 5: Ch1, 1sc in each of next 2 sc, 2sc in next sc, [1sc in each of next 3 sc, 2sc in next sc] to end, join with a sl st. (*20 sts*)

Rounds 6–8: Ch1, 1sc in next sc, 1sc in each sc to end, join with a sl st.

Round 9: Ch1, 1sc in each of next 2 sc, sc2tog, [1sc in each of next 3 sc, sc2tog] to end, join with a sl st. (*16 sts*)

Round 10: Change to A, ch1, 1scBLO in next sc, 1scBLO in each sc to end, join with a sl st.

Rounds 11–25: Ch1, 1sc in next sc, 1sc in each sc to end, join with a sl st.

Fasten off.

END OF BOOT

(make 2)

Round 1: Using B, ch4, join with a sl st to form a ring.

Round 2: Ch1 (counts as first sc), 7sc in ring, join with a sl st. (*8 sts*)

Round 3: Ch1, 2sc in next sc, [1sc in next sc, 2sc in next sc] to end, join with a sl st. (*12 sts*)

Round 4: Ch1, 1sc in next sc, 2sc in next sc, [1sc in each of next 2 sc, 2sc in next sc] to end, join with a sl st. (*16 sts*)

Round 5: Ch1, 1sc in each of next 2 sc, 2sc in next sc, [1sc in each of next 3 sc, 2sc in next sc] to end, join with a sl st. (*20 sts*)

Rounds 6 and 7: Ch1, 1sc in next sc, 1sc in each sc to end, join with a sl st.

Fasten off.

HAT

Round 1: Using B, ch5, join with a sl st to form a ring.

Round 2: Ch3 (counts as first dc), 11dc in ring, join with a sl st. (*12 sts*)

Round 3: Ch3, 1dc in same dc, 2dc in each dc to end, join with a sl st. (*24 sts*)

Round 4: Ch3, 2dc in next dc [1dc in next dc, 2dc in next dc] to end, join with a sl st. (*36 sts*)

Round 5: Ch3, 1dcBLO in next dc, 1dcBLO in each dc to end, join with a sl st.

Round 6: Ch3, 1dc in next dc, 1dc in each dc to end, join with a sl st.

Fasten off.

TAIL

Row 1: Using A, ch7.
Row 2: 1sc in 2nd ch from hook (missed ch does not count as sc), 1sc in each ch to end. (*6 sts*)
Row 3: Ch1 (counts as first sc), 1sc in next sc, 1sc in each sc to end.
Rep Row 3 until work measures approx. 10in (25.5cm). Fasten off.

SKIRT

Join B in front loop of center back st of Round 22 of body.
Round 1: Ch3 (counts as first dc), 1dc in next sc, 1dc in each sc to end, join with a sl st. (*48 sts*)
Round 2: Ch3, 2dc in next dc, [1dc in next dc, 2dc in next dc] to end, join with a sl st. (72 *sts*)
Round 3: Ch3, 1dc in next dc, 1dc in each dc to end, join with a sl st.
Round 4: Ch3, 1dc in next dc, 2dc in next dc, [1dc in each of next 2 dc, 2dc in next dc] to end, join with a sl st. (*96 sts*)
Round 5: Ch3, 1dc in next dc, 1dc in each dc to end, join with a sl st.
Fasten off.

PURSE

Row 1: Using B, ch8.
Row 2: 1sc in 2nd ch from hook (missed ch does not count as sc), 1sc in each ch to end. (7 *sts*)
Rows 3–10: Ch1 (counts as first sc), 1sc in next sc, 1sc in each sc to end.
Ch15 for handle.
Fasten off.

TO MAKE UP

Insert the safety eyes in the head in the positions required, using the photo as a guide, and secure with the backs (see page 141). Stuff the head. To form the two puffed parts of the snout, stuff the snout lightly then wind the yarn end around the center and secure firmly at the back with a stitch. Using E, embroider mouth markings onto the snout. Push the post of the safety nose through the crochet above the mouth markings and secure with the back. Sew the snout to the head, using the photo as a guide for positioning. Stuff the base of the snout lightly and sew to the head below the snout.

Place the inner ear on top of the outer ear and join with a single crochet seam (see page 140) all around using A.

Sew the ear to one side of the head. Lightly stuff the inside of the hat and sew to the other side of the head. Sew the head to the body.

Stuff the legs and the ends of the boots. Sew the ends of the boots to the end of each leg, then sew the legs to the body.

Stuff the arms. For each arm, flatten the opening at the top and sew it closed so that the arms will hang down. Sew the arms to the body.

Fold the tail in half lengthwise and sew the seam, then sew the tail to back of body in position required.

Fold the purse in half and sew a seam on both sides leaving the top open. Sew the end of the chain to the other side at the top of the bag to form the handle. Sew the purse to the paw of the cat.

Add any extra embellishments to decorate your cat. If you are using D for edging decoration as in the photos you will need to cut the lengths required and glue into position.

What a great project to create for that special little someone! This simple and charming character is crocheted in single crochet stitch throughout, making him a perfect project for someone new to crochet. If you're giving Christopher to a young child, omit the safety eyes and nose and embroider these features instead (see page 141).

christopher the snuggle cat

YARN AND MATERIALS
King Cole Big Value Chunky (100% acrylic), bulky (chunky) weight yarn, 167yd (152m) per 3½oz (100g) ball
¾ ball of shade 824 Blue (A)
½ ball of shade 546 Caramel (B)
⅓ ball of shade 553 Red (C)

King Cole Hedgerow Chunky (100% acrylic), bulky (chunky) weight yarn, 332yd (304m) per 7oz (200g) ball
¼ ball of shade 5841 Thicket (D)

King Cole Glitz DK (97% acrylic, 5% polyester), light worsted (DK) weight yarn, 317yd (290m) per 1¾oz (50g) ball
½ ball of shade 565 Silver (E)

Small amount of black light worsted (DK) weight yarn (F)

20mm pink safety nose

Pair of 20mm safety eyes

Toy fiberfill

HOOK AND EQUIPMENT
US E-4 (3.5mm) and US H-8 (5mm) crochet hooks
Yarn needle

FINISHED SIZE
Standing 18in (46cm)

ABBREVIATIONS
See page 142.

PATTERN NOTE
If giving the cat to a young child, substitute the safety eyes and nose with embroidery in yarn (see page 141).

BODY
Round 1: Using US H-8 (5mm) hook and A, ch5, join with a sl st to form a ring.
Round 2: Ch3 (counts as first dc), 11dc in ring, join with a sl st. (*12 sts*)
Round 3: Ch3, 1dc in same dc, 2dc in each dc to end, join with a sl st. (*24 sts*)
Round 4: Ch3, 2dc in next dc, [1dc in next dc, 2dc in next dc] to end, join with a sl st. (*36 sts*)
Round 5: Ch1 (counts as first sc), 1sc in next dc, 1sc in each dc to end, join with a sl st.
Round 6: Ch1, 1scBLO in next sc, 1scBLO in each sc to end, join with a sl st.
Rounds 7–19: Ch1, 1sc in next sc, 1sc in each sc to end, join with a sl st.
Round 20: Change to D, ch1, 1scBLO in next sc, 1scBLO in each sc to end, join with a sl st.
Rounds 21–25: Ch1, 1sc in next sc, 1sc in each sc to end, join with a sl st.
Round 26: Ch1, sc2tog, [1sc in next sc, sc2tog] to end, join with a sl st. (*24 sts*)
Round 27: Ch1, 1sc in next sc, sc2tog, [1sc in each of next 2 sc, sc2tog] to end, join with a sl st. (*18 sts*)
Round 28: Ch1, sc2tog, [1sc in next sc, sc2tog] to end, join with a sl st. (*12 sts*)
Fasten off, leaving a length of yarn.
Stuff body firmly. Thread end onto needle, gather remaining sts together, fasten off.

HEAD
Round 1: Using US H-8 (5mm) hook and B, ch4, join with a sl st to form a ring.
Round 2: Ch1 (counts as first sc), 7sc in ring, join with a sl st. (*8 sts*)
Round 3: Ch1, 1sc in same sc, 2sc in each sc to end, join with a sl st. (*16 sts*)

Round 4: Ch1, 2sc in next sc, [1sc in next sc, 2sc in next sc] to end, join with a sl st. (*24 sts*)

Round 5: Ch1, 1sc in next sc, 1sc in each sc to end, join with a sl st.

Round 6: Ch1, 1sc in each of next 4 sc, 2sc in next sc, [1sc in each of next 5 sc, 2sc in next sc] to end, join with a sl st. (*28 sts*)

Round 7: Ch1, 1sc in each of next 5 sc, 2sc in next sc, [1sc in each of next 6 sc, 2sc in next sc] to end, join with a sl st. (*32 sts*)

Round 8: Ch1, 1sc in each of next 2 sc, 2sc in next sc, [1sc in each of next 3 sc, 2sc in next sc] to end, join with a sl st. (*40 sts*)

Rounds 9–12: Ch1, 1sc in next sc, 1sc in each sc to end, join with a sl st.

Round 13: Ch1, 1sc in each of next 2 sc, sc2tog, [1sc in each of next 3 sc, sc2tog] to end join with a sl st. (*32 sts*)

Round 14: Ch1, 1sc in next sc, sc2tog, [1sc in each of next 2 sc, sc2tog] to end, join with a sl st. (*24 sts*)

Round 15: Ch1, sc2tog, [1sc in next sc, sc2tog] to end, join with a sl st. (*16 sts*)

Round 16: Ch1, 1sc in next sc, 1sc in each sc to end, join with a sl st.
Fasten off.

SNOUT

Round 1: Using US H-8 (5mm) hook and B, ch4, join with a sl st to form a ring.

Round 2: Ch1 (counts as first sc), 7sc in ring, join with a sl st. (*8 sts*)

Round 3: Ch1, 2sc in next sc, [1sc in next sc, 2sc in next sc] to end, join with a sl st. (*12 sts*)

Round 4: Ch1, 1sc in next sc, 1sc in each sc to end, join with a sl st.
Fasten off.

EARS

(make 2)

Row 1: Using US H-8 (5mm) hook and B, ch2.

Row 2: 1sc in 2nd ch from hook (missed ch does not count as sc). (*1 st*)

Row 3: Ch1 (counts as first sc), 1sc in same sc. (*2 sts*)

Row 4: Ch1, 1sc in same sc, 1sc in next sc. (*3 sts*)

Row 5: Ch1, 1sc in same sc, 1sc in each sc to end. (*4 sts*)

Row 6: Ch1, 1sc in same sc, 1sc in each sc to end. (*5 sts*)
Fasten off.

ARMS

(make 2)

Round 1: Using US H-8 (5mm) hook and B, ch4, join with a sl st to form a ring.

Round 2: Ch1 (counts as first sc), 7sc in ring, join with a sl st. (*8 sts*)

Round 3: Ch1, 2sc in next sc, [1sc in next sc, 2sc in next sc] to end, join with a sl st. (*12 sts*)

Rounds 4 and 5: Ch1, 1sc in next sc, 1sc in each sc to end, join with a sl st.

Round 6: Change to A, ch1, 1scBLO in next sc, 1scBLO in each sc to end, join with a sl st.

Rounds 7–16: Ch1, 1sc in next sc, 1sc in each sc to end, join with a sl st.

Fasten off.

LEGS

(make 2)

Round 1: Using US H-8 (5mm) hook and B, ch5, join with a sl st to form a ring. (*5 sts*)

Round 2: Ch1 (counts as first sc), 9sc in ring, join with a sl st. (*10 sts*)

Round 3: Ch1, 1sc in each of next 2 sc, [2sc in next sc] twice, 1sc in each of next 3 sc, [2sc in next sc] twice, join with a sl st. (*14 sts*)

Round 4: Ch1, 1sc in each of next 4 sc, [2sc in next sc] twice, 1sc in each of next 5 sc, [2sc in next sc] twice, join with a sl st. (*18 sts*)

Round 5: Ch1, 1sc in each of next 6 sc, [2sc in next sc] twice, 1sc in each of next 7 sc, [2sc in next sc] twice, join with a sl st. (*22 sts*)

Rounds 6 and 7: Ch1, 1sc in next sc, 1sc in each sc to end, join with a sl st.

Round 8: Ch1, sc2tog, [1sc in next st, sc2tog] 3 times, 1sc in each sc to end, join with a sl st. (*18 sts*)

Round 9: Ch1, sc2tog, [1sc in next st, sc2tog] twice, 1sc in each sc to end, join with a sl st. (*15 sts*)

Fasten off B, change to D.

Rounds 10–18: Ch1, 1sc in next sc, 1sc in each sc to end, join with a sl st.

Fasten off.

SCARF

Row 1: Using US H-8 (5mm) hook and C, ch8.

Row 2: 1dc in 3rd ch from hook (missed 2 ch do not count as dc), 1dc in each ch to end. (*6 sts*)

Row 3: Ch3 (counts as first dc), 1dc in next dc, 1dc in each dc to end.

Rep Row 3 until you reach length required.

Fasten off.

FISH

Round 1: Using 3.5mm (US E-4) hook and E, ch3, join with a sl st to form a ring.

Round 2: Ch1 (counts as first sc), 5sc in ring, join with a sl st. (*6 sts*)

Round 3: Ch1, 2sc in next sc, [1sc in next sc, 2sc in next sc] to end, join with a sl st. (*9 sts*)

Round 4: Ch1, 1sc in next sc, 1sc in each sc to end, join with a sl st.

Round 5: Ch1, 1sc in next sc, 2sc in next sc, [1sc in each of next 2 sc, 2sc in next sc] to end, join with a sl st. (*12 sts*)

Rounds 6–12: Ch1, 1sc in next sc, 1sc in each sc to end, join with a sl st.

Round 13: Ch1, 1sc in next sc, sc2tog, [1sc in each of next 2 sc, sc2tog] to end, join with a sl st. (*9 sts*)

Round 14: Ch1, 1sc in next sc, 1sc in each sc to end, join with a sl st.

Stuff fish firmly.

Round 15: Ch1, sc2tog, [1sc in next sc, sc2tog] to end, join with a sl st. (*6 sts*)

Round 16: Ch1, 1sc in next sc, 1sc in each sc to end, join with a sl st.

Flatten piece and work through both layers on next row to form tail:

Row 17: Ch3, (1dc, ch3, 1sc) in next st, sl st in next st, ch3, (1dc, ch3, 1sc) in next st.

Fasten off.

TO MAKE UP

Using F, embroider the mouth markings on the snout.

Add the safety nose using the photo as a guide for positioning and secure with the back. Sew short lengths of B to the snout for the whiskers. Stuff the snout and sew to the head. Add the safety eyes to the head above the snout and secure with the backs (see page 141). Stuff the head firmly. Sew the ears onto the head using the photos as a guide for positioning.

Sew the head to the body. Stuff the arms and sew to either side of the body. Stuff the legs and sew to the bottom of the body. Embroider claws onto the feet using F.

Cut lengths of C approx. 6in (15cm) long to make a fringe for the scarf, then trim to the length required. Add the scarf around the neck.

Tuck the fish under one arm and sew in position.

SKILL RATING ● ● ●

YARN AND MATERIALS
King Cole Moments DK (100% polyester), light worsted (DK) weight yarn, 98yd (90m) per 1¾oz (50g) ball
  ¾ ball of shade 470 White (A)

King Cole Truffle Glitz DK (91% polyamide, 9% glitter), light worsted (DK) weight yarn, 170yd (156m) per 3½oz (100g) ball
  10g of shade 5420 Snow White (B)

King Cole Glitz DK (97% acrylic, 5% polyester), light worsted (DK) weight yarn, 317yd (290m) per 1¾oz (50g) ball
  1 ball of shade 481 Cherry (C)
  ⅜oz (10g) of shade 565 Silver (D)
  ¾oz (20g) of shade 483 Diamond White (E)

Small amount of black light worsted (DK) weight yarn (F)

Small amount of white King Cole Super Yummy or similar chenille yarn (optional) (G)

Pair of 14mm safety eyes

15mm pink safety nose

Toy fiberfill

Embellishments of your choice

HOOK AND EQUIPMENT
US H-8 (5mm) and US G-6 (4mm) crochet hooks

Stitch marker

Yarn needle

FINISHED SIZE
17in (43cm) standing

ABBREVIATIONS
See page 142.

PATTERN NOTE
It is advisable to use a stitch marker with this pattern.
If giving the cat to a young child, substitute the embellisments and the safety eyes and nose with embroidery in yarn (see page 141).

This charming nutcracker will be the center of attention and will brighten up any Christmas display. It would also make a great gift for the holiday season. If you're giving this cat to a young child, embroider the nose and eyes with yarn instead of using the safety nose and eyes. Crocheted in single crochet using a festive light worsted yarn with a unique sparkle, this will be a real head-turner.

nutcracker cat

HEAD
Round 1: Using US H-8 (5mm) hook and A, ch4, join with a sl st to form a ring.
Round 2: Ch1 (counts as first sc), 7sc in ring, join with a sl st. (*8 sts*)
Round 3: Ch1, 1sc in same sc, 2sc in each sc to end, join with a sl st. (*16 sts*)
Round 4: Ch1, 2sc in next sc, [1sc in each of next 2 sc, 2sc in next sc] to end, join with a sl st. (*24 sts*)
Round 5: Ch1, 1sc in next sc, 1sc in each sc to end, join with a sl st.
Round 6: Ch1, 1sc in each of next 4 sc, 2sc in next sc, [1sc in each of next 5 sc, 2sc in next sc] to end, join with a sl st. (*28 sts*)
Rounds 7–10: Ch1, 1sc in next sc, 1sc in each sc to end, join with a sl st.
Round 11: Ch1, 1sc in next sc, sc2tog, [1sc in each of next 2 sc, sc2tog] to end, join with a sl st. (*21 sts*)
Round 12: Ch1, sc2tog, [1sc in next sc, sc2tog] to end, join with a sl st. (*14 sts*)
Fasten off.

SNOUT
Round 1: Using US G-6 (4mm) hook and B, ch4, join with a sl st to form a ring.
Round 2: Ch1 (counts as first sc), 7sc in ring, join with a sl st. (*8 sts*)
Round 3: Ch1, 2sc in next sc, [1sc in next sc, 2sc in next sc] to end, join with a sl st. (*12 sts*)
Round 4: Ch1, 1sc in next sc, 1sc in each sc to end, join with a sl st.
Fasten off.

Round 5: Ch1, 1sc in next sc, 2sc in next sc, [1sc in each of next 2 sc, 2sc in next sc] to end, join with a sl st. (*32 sts*)

Round 6: Ch1, 1sc in each of next 2 sc, 2sc in next sc, [1sc in each of next 3 sc, 2sc in next sc] to end, join with a sl st. (*40 sts*)

Round 7: Ch1, 1sc in each of next 3 sc, 2sc in next sc, [1sc in each of next 4 sc, 2sc in next sc] to end, join with a sl st. (*48 sts*)

Round 8: Ch1, 1sc in each of next 4 sc, 2sc in next sc, [1sc in each of next 5 sc, 2sc in next sc] to end, join with a sl st. (*56 sts*)

Round 9: Ch1, 1scBLO in next sc, 1scBLO in each sc to end, join with a sl st.

Rounds 10–13: Ch1, 1sc in next sc, 1sc in each sc to end, join with a sl st.

Round 14: Ch1, 1scBLO in next sc, 1scBLO in each sc to end, join with a sl st.

Rounds 15–32: Ch1, 1sc in next sc, 1sc in each sc to end, join with a sl st.

Round 33: Ch1, 1sc in each of next 4 sc, sc2tog, [1sc in each of next 5 sc, sc2tog] to end, join with a sl st. (*48 sts*)

Round 34: Ch1, 1sc in each of next 3 sc, sc2tog, [1sc in each of next 4 sc, sc2tog] to end, join with a sl st. (*40 sts*)

Round 35: Ch1, 1sc in each of next 2 sc, sc2tog, [1sc in each of next 3 sc, sc2tog] to end, join with a sl st. (*32 sts*)

Round 36: Ch1, 1sc in next sc, sc2tog, [1sc in each of next 2 sc, sc2tog] to end, join with a sl st. (*24 sts*)

Round 37: Ch1, sc2tog, [1sc in next sc, sc2tog] to end, join with a sl st. (*16 sts*)
Fasten off.

EARS

(make 2)

Row 1: Using US H-8 (5mm) hook and A, ch2.

Row 2: 1sc in 2nd ch from hook (missed ch does not count as sc). (*1 st*)

Row 3: Ch1 (counts as first sc), 1sc in same sc. (*2 sts*)

Row 4: Ch1, 1sc in same sc, 1sc in next sc. (*3 sts*)

Rows 5 and 6: Ch1, 1sc in each of next 2 sc.
Fasten off.

BODY

Work from bottom upward.

Round 1: Using US G-6 (4mm) hook and C, ch4, join with a sl st to form a ring.

Round 2: Ch1 (counts as first sc), 7sc in ring, join with a sl st. (*8 sts*)

Round 3: Ch1, 1sc in same sc, 2sc in each sc to end, join with a sl st. (*16 sts*)

Round 4: Ch1, 2sc in next sc, [1sc in next sc, 2sc in next sc, join with a sl st. (*24 sts*)

BELT

Row 1: Using US G-6 (4mm) hook and D, ch33.

Row 2: 1sc in 2nd ch from hook (missed ch does not count as sc), 1sc in each ch to end. (*32 sts*)
Fasten off.

BOTTOM OF JACKET

Using US G-6 (4mm) hook and C, join yarn in front loop of center back st of Round 14 of body.

Row 1: Ch3 (counts as first dc), [2dc in next sc, 1dc in next sc] to last st, turn, leaving one sc unworked. (*83 sts*)

Row 2: Ch3, 1dc in next dc, 1dc in each dc to end.
Fasten off.

ARMS

(make 2)

Round 1: Using US G-6 (4mm) hook and E, ch4, join with a sl st to form a ring.

Round 2: Ch1 (counts as first sc), 7sc in ring, join with a sl st. (*8 sts*)

Round 3: Ch1, 1sc in same sc, 2sc in each sc to end, join with a sl st. (*16 sts*)

Rounds 4 and 5: Ch1, 1sc in next sc, 1sc in each sc to end, join with a sl st.

Round 6: Change to C, ch1, 1scBLO in next sc, 1scBLO in each sc to end, join with a sl st.

Rounds 7–18: Ch1, 1sc in next sc, 1sc in each sc to end, join with a sl st.

Stuff firmly.

Round 19: Change to E, ch1, 1scBLO in next sc, 1scBLO in each sc to end, join with a sl st.

Round 20: Ch1, 1sc in next sc, 1sc in each sc to end, join with a sl st.

Round 21: Ch1, 1sc in next sc, sc2tog, [1sc in each of next 2 sc, sc2tog] to end, join with a sl st. (*12 sts*)

Continue to stuff firmly.

Round 22: Ch1, sc2tog, [1sc in next sc, sc2tog] to end, join with a sl st. (*8 sts*)

Fasten off, leaving a length of yarn.

Thread yarn end onto needle, gather remaining sts together, fasten off.

COLLAR

Row 1: Using US G-6 (4mm) hook and F, ch28.

Row 2: 1sc in 2nd ch from hook (missed ch does not count as sc), 1sc in each ch to end. (*27 sts*)

Row 3: Ch1 (counts as first sc), 1sc in next sc, 1sc in each sc to end.

Fasten off.

LEGS AND BOOTS

(make 2)

Round 1: Using US G-6 (4mm) hook and C, ch4, join with a sl st to form a ring.

Round 2: Ch1 (counts as first sc), 7sc in ring, join with a sl st to first sc. (*8 sts*)

Round 3: Ch1, 2sc in next sc, [1sc in next sc, 2sc in next sc] to end, join with a sl st. (*12 sts*)

Round 4: Ch1, 2sc in next sc, [1sc in next sc, 2sc in next sc] to end, join with a sl st. (*18 sts*)

Round 5: Ch1, 1scBLO in next sc, 1scBLO in each sc to end, join with a sl st.

Rounds 6–14: Ch1, 1sc in next sc, 1sc in each sc to end, join with a sl st.

Stuff firmly.

Round 15: Change to E, ch1, 1scBLO in next sc, 1scBLO in each sc to end, join with a sl st.

Rounds 16–35: Ch1, 1sc in next sc, 1sc in each sc to end, join with a sl st.

Fasten off.

Stuff firmly.

END OF BOOT

(make 2)

Round 1: Using US G-6 (4mm) hook and C, ch4, join with a sl st to form a ring.

Round 2: Ch1 (counts as first sc), 7sc in ring, join with a sl st. (*8 sts*)

Round 3: Ch1, 2sc in next sc, [1sc in next sc, 2sc in next sc] to end, join with a sl st. (*12 sts*)

Round 4: Ch1, 1sc in next sc, 1sc in each sc to end, join with a sl st.

Round 5: Ch1, 1sc in next sc, 2sc in next sc, [1sc in each of next 2 sc, 2sc in next sc] to end, join with a sl st. (*16 sts*)

Rounds 6–8: Ch1, 1sc in next sc, 1sc in each sc to end, join with a sl st.

Round 9: Ch1, 1sc in each of next 2 sc, 2sc in next sc, [1sc in each of next 3 sc, 2sc in next sc] to end, join with a sl st. (*20 sts*)

Fasten off.

HAT

Round 1: Using US G-6 (4mm) hook and C, ch4, join with a sl st to form a ring.

Round 2: Ch1 (counts as first sc), 7sc in ring, join with a sl st. (*8 sts*)

Round 3: Ch1, 1sc in next sc, 1sc in each sc to end, join with a sl st.

Round 4: Ch1, 2sc in next sc, [1sc in next sc, 2sc in next sc] to end, join with a sl st. (*12 sts*)

Rounds 5–7: Ch1, 1sc in next sc, 1sc in each sc to end, join with a sl st.

Round 8: Change to B, ch1, 1sc in next sc, 2sc in next sc, [1sc in each of next 2 sc, 2sc in next sc] to end, join with a sl st. (*16 sts*)

Fasten off.

TO MAKE UP

Stuff the body firmly.

Add the nose to the snout and secure with the safety back, then stuff the snout firmly. Embroider the mouth markings using F. Sew the snout to the head using the photos as a guide for positioning. Add the eyes to head and secure with the safety backs. Stuff the head firmly, then sew ears to either side of the head using the photos as a guide for positioning. Sew the head to the body. Stuff the hat and sew it to the head. Wrap the collar around the neck and secure it with a few stitches.

Wrap the belt around the body and secure it with a few stitches. Embroider the belt buckle with a short length of F.

Sew the arms to the body with the top of each of arm in line with the shoulders. Stuff the ends of the boots and sew to the front of each leg at the bottom to form the boots. If you'd like your nutcracker to be sitting, fold the top of the leg in half and join the seam (see page 139). If you'd like the nutcracker to be standing, leave the leg gap open. Sew the legs to the bottom of the body.

If you are using G for edging decoration as in the photos, cut the lengths required and glue into position around bottom of the jacket and sleeves. Add any extra embellishments to decorate your nutcracker.

ballerina cat

How graceful this little cat looks with her pretty outfit! She would be a perfect gift for the little girl in your life and would also make a lovely Christmas tree topper. This ballet-dancing cat is crocheted in simple single crochet stitch throughout.

SKILL RATING ● ● ○

YARN AND MATERIALS
King Cole Baby Alpaca DK (100% baby alpaca), light worsted (DK) weight yarn, 110yd (100m) per 1¾oz (50g) ball
  ¾ ball of Koala shade 504 (A)

King Cole Glitz DK (97% acrylic, 3% polyester), light worsted (DK) weight yarn, 317yd (290m) per 3½oz (100g) ball
  ½ ball of Christmas shade 1698 (B)
  Small amounts of:
  Diamond White shade 483 (C)
  Pink shade 4721 (D)

Small amount of black light worsted (DK) weight yarn (E)

Toy fiberfill

Pair of 12mm cat safety eyes

Embellishments for decoration

HOOK AND EQUIPMENT
US G-6 (4mm) crochet hook

Yarn needle

FINISHED SIZE
Standing approx. 14in (35.5cm)

ABBREVIATIONS
See page 142.

PATTERN NOTE
If giving the cat to a young child, substitute the embellisments and the safety eyes and nose with embroidery in yarn (see page 141).

BODY

Round 1: Using B, ch4, join with a sl st to form a ring.
Round 2: Ch1 (counts as first sc), 7sc in ring, join with a sl st. (*8 sts*)
Round 3: Ch1, 1sc in same sc, 2sc in each sc to end, join with a sl st. (*16 sts*)
Round 4: Ch1, 2sc in next sc, [1sc in next sc, 2sc in next sc] to end, join with a sl st. (*24 sts*)
Round 5: Ch1, 1sc in same sc, [2sc in next sc] twice, 1sc in each of next 9 sc, [2sc in next sc] 3 times, 1sc in each of next 9 sc, join with a sl st. (*30 sts*)
Round 6: Ch1, 1sc in same sc, [2sc in next sc] twice, 1sc in each of next 12 sc, [2 sc in next sc] 3 times, 1sc in each of next 12 sc, join with a sl st. (*36 sts*)
Round 7: Ch1, 1sc in same sc, 2sc in next sc, 1sc in each of next 16 sc, [2sc in next sc] twice, 1sc in each of next 16 sc, join with a sl st. (*40 sts*)
Round 8: Ch1, 1scBLO in next sc, 1scBLO in each sc to end, join with a sl st.
Rounds 9-14: Ch1, 1sc in next sc, 1sc in each sc to end, join with a sl st.
Round 15: Ch1, 1scBLO in next sc, 1scBLO in each sc to end, join with a sl st.
Rounds 16-26: Ch1, 1sc in next sc, 1sc in each sc to end, join with a sl st.
Fasten off B, join in A.
Round 27: Ch1, 1scBLO in next sc, 1scBLO in each sc to end, join with a sl st.
Round 28: Ch1, 1sc in next sc, 1sc in each sc to end, join with a sl st.

Round 29: Ch1, 1sc in next sc, sc2tog, [1sc in each of next 2 sc, sc2tog] to end, join with a sl st. (*30 sts*)
Round 30: [Sc2tog] 3 times, 1sc in each of next 9 sc, [sc2tog] 3 times, 1sc in each of next 9 sc, join with a sl st. (*24 sts*)
Round 31: [Sc2tog] 3 times, 1sc in each of next 6 sc, [sc2tog] 3 times, 1sc in each of next 6 sc, join with a sl st. (*18 sts*)
Fasten off, leaving a length of yarn.
Stuff body firmly.
Thread a needle with yarn end, flatten the opening and sew it closed.

SKIRT

Join B in front loop of any st in Round 15 of main body.
Round 1: Ch3 (counts as first dc), 1dc in same sc, 2dc in each sc to end, join with a sl st. (*80 sts*)
Rounds 2-5: Ch3, 1dc in next dc, 1dc in each dc to end, join with a sl st.
Fasten off B, join in C.
Round 6: Ch1 (counts as first sc), 2sc in next sc, [1sc in next sc, 2sc in next sc] to end, join with a sl st. (*120 sts*)
Fasten off.

SHOULDER STRAPS

(make 2)
Row 1: Using B, ch12.
Fasten off.

HEAD

Round 1: Using A, ch4, join with a sl st to form a ring.
Round 2: Ch1 (counts as first sc), 7sc in ring, join with a sl st. (*8 sts*)
Rounds 3 and 4: Ch1, 1sc in next sc, 1sc in each sc to end, join with a sl st.
Round 5: Ch1, 2sc in next sc, [1sc in next sc, 2sc in next sc] to end, join with a sl st. (*12 sts*)
Round 6: Ch1, 1sc in next sc, 1sc in each sc to end, join with a sl st.
Round 7: Ch1, 2sc in next sc, [1sc in next sc, 2sc in next sc] to end, join with a sl st. (*18 sts*)
Round 8: Ch1, 1sc in each of next 2 sc, [2sc in next sc] 12 times, 1sc in each of next 3 sc, join with a sl st. (*30 sts*)
Round 9: Ch1, 1sc in next sc, 1sc in each sc to end, join with a sl st.
Round 10: Ch1, 1sc in same sc, [2sc in next sc] twice, 1sc in each of next 12 sc, [2sc in next sc] 3 times, 1sc in each of next 12 sc, join with a sl st. (*36 sts*)
Rounds 11-15: Ch1, 1sc in next sc, 1sc in each sc to end, join with a sl st.

Round 16: Ch1, 1sc in each of next 3 sc, sc2tog, [1sc in each of next 4 sc, sc2tog] to end, join with a sl st. (*30 sts*)

Round 17: Ch1, 1sc in next sc, 1sc in each sc to end, join with a sl st.

Round 18: Ch1, 1sc in each of next 2 sc, sc2tog, [1sc in each of next 3 sc, sc2tog] to end, join with a sl st. (*24 sts*)

Round 19: [Sc2tog] to end, join with a sl st. (*12 sts*)
Fasten off, leaving a length of yarn.

INNER EARS
(make 2)
Row 1: Using D, ch2.
Row 2: 1sc in 2nd ch from hook (missed ch does not count as sc). (*1 st*)
Row 3: Ch1 (counts as first sc), 1sc in same sc. (*2 sts*)
Row 4: Ch1, 1sc in same sc, 1sc in next sc to end. (*3 sts*)
Row 5: Ch1, 1sc in same sc, 1sc in each sc to end. (*4 sts*)
Row 6: Ch1, 1sc in same sc, 1sc in each sc to end. (*5 sts*)
Fasten off.

OUTER EARS
(make 2)
Row 1: Using A, ch2.
Row 2: 1sc in 2nd ch from hook (missed ch does not count as sc). (*1 st*)
Row 3: Ch1 (counts as first sc), 1sc in same sc. (*2 sts*)
Row 4: Ch1, 1sc in same sc, 1sc in next sc to end. (*3 sts*)
Row 5: Ch1, 1sc in same sc, 1sc in each sc to end. (*4 sts*)
Row 6: Ch1, 1sc in same sc, 1sc in each sc to end. (*5 sts*)
Fasten off.

ARMS
(make 2)
Round 1: Using A, ch4, join with a sl st to form a ring.
Round 2: Ch1 (counts as first sc), 7sc in ring, join with a sl st. (*8 sts*)
Rounds 3–18: Ch1, 1sc in next sc, 1sc in each sc to end, join with a sl st.
Fasten off.

LEGS
(make 2)
Round 1: Using C, ch4, join with a sl st to form a ring.
Round 2: Ch1 (counts as first sc), 7sc in ring, join with a sl st. (*8 sts*)
Rounds 3–8: Ch1, 1sc in next sc, 1sc in each sc to end, join with a sl st.
Fasten off C, join in A.

Round 9: Ch1, 1scBLO in next sc, 1scBLO in each sc to end, join with a sl st.
Rounds 10–28: Ch1, 1sc in next sc, 1sc in each sc to end, join with a sl st.
Fasten off.

TO MAKE UP
Add the safety eyes using the photo as a guide for positioning and secure with the backs (see page 141). Stuff the head firmly. Thread the yarn end onto a needle, gather the remaining sts together and fasten off. Using D, embroider the nose with satin stitch. Using E, embroider the mouth. Place an inner ear on top of an outer ear and using A work a single crochet seam (see page 140) through both layers to join. Repeat for the second ear, then sew the ears to the head.

Sew the head and arms to the body. Sew straps to each side of bodice and over the shoulders.

Sew the legs to the body. To make the straps for the ballet shoes, sew two short lengths of C to the back of the ballet shoe. Wrap the lengths around the bottom of the leg a couple of times following the photograph and tie with a knot at the back of the leg.

If you are using as a Christmas tree topper, add two short lengths of yarn to the back of the body to tie to the tree.

Add any embellishments (optional).

Crocheted in single crochet stitch throughout, this soft and fluffy cat is perfect for showing off to all cat lovers. If you're giving Charlie to a young child, leave out the safety eyes and nose and embroider them instead. What more could any cat owner ask for than this luxuriously soft cuddle pal?

charlie the fluffy cat

SKILL RATING ● ● ○

YARN AND MATERIALS
King Cole Velveteen (100% polyester), super bulky (super chunky) weight yarn, 71yd (65m) per 3½oz (100g) ball
   4 balls of Snow shade 6120 (A)

King Cole Big Value Chunky (100% acrylic), bulky (chunky) weight yarn, 167yd (152m) per 3½oz (100g) ball
   ⅓ ball of Blue Heaven shade 559 (B)

Small amount of gray light worsted (DK) weight yarn (C)

Pair of 20mm cat safety eyes

20mm pink cat safety nose

Toy fiberfill

HOOK AND EQUIPMENT
US H-8 (5mm) crochet hook
Yarn needle

FINISHED SIZE
Sitting 13in (33cm)

PATTERN NOTE
It is advisable to use a stitch marker with the Velveteen yarn. If giving the cat to a young child, substitute the the safety eyes and nose with embroidery in yarn (see page 141).

ABBREVIATIONS
See page 142.

BODY
Round 1: Using A, ch5, join with a sl st to form a ring.
Round 2: Ch1 (counts as first sc), 11sc in ring, join with a sl st. (*12 sts*)
Round 3: Ch1, 1sc in same sc, 2sc in each sc to end, join with a sl st. (*24 sts*)
Round 4: Ch1, 1sc in next sc, 1sc in each sc to end, join with a sl st.
Round 5: Ch1, 1sc in next sc, 2sc in next sc, [1sc in each of next 2 sc, 2sc in next sc] to end, join with a sl st. (*32 sts*)
Rounds 6–18: Ch1, 1sc in next sc, 1sc in each sc to end, join with a sl st.
Round 19: Ch1, 1sc in next sc, sc2tog, [1sc in each of next 2 sc, sc2tog] to end, join with a sl st. (*24 sts*)
Round 20: Ch1, sc2tog, [1sc in next sc, sc2tog] to end, join with a sl st. (*16 sts*)
Stuff body firmly before cont.
Round 21: [Sc2tog] to end, join with a sl st. (*8 sts*)
Fasten off, leaving a length of yarn. Thread yarn end onto needle, gather remaining sts together, fasten off.

HEAD
Round 1: Using A, ch4, join with a sl st to form a ring. (*4 sts*)
Round 2: Ch1 (counts as first sc), 7sc in ring, join with a sl st. (*8 sts*)
Round 3: Ch1, 1sc in same sc, 2sc in each sc to end, join with a sl st. (*16 sts*)
Round 4: Ch1, 2sc in next sc, [1sc in next sc, 2sc in next sc] to end, join with a sl st. (*24 sts*)
Round 5: Ch1, 1sc in next sc, 1sc in each sc to end, join with a sl st.
Round 6: Ch1, 1sc in each of next 2 sc, 2sc in next sc, [1sc in each of next 3 sc, 2sc in next sc] to end, join with a sl st. (*30 sts*)
Rounds 7–11: Ch1, 1sc in next sc, 1sc in each sc to end, join with a sl st.
Round 12: Ch1, sc2tog, [1sc in next sc, sc2tog] to end, join with a sl st. (*20 sts*)

Round 13: Ch1, 1sc in each of next 2 sc, sc2tog, [1sc in each of next 3 sc, sc2tog] to end, join with a sl st. (*16 sts*)
Round 14: Ch1, 1sc in next sc, sc2tog, [1sc in each of next 2 sc, sc2tog] to end, join with a sl st. (*12 sts*)
Fasten off, leaving a length of yarn.

SNOUT
Round 1: Using A, ch5.
Round 2: 1sc in 2nd ch from hook (missed ch does not count as sc), 1sc in each ch to last ch, 3sc in last ch, working along bottom of chain, 1sc in each ch to end, 1sc in end of row, join with a sl st. (*10 sts*)
Round 3: Ch1 (counts as first sc), 1sc in next sc, 1sc in each sc to end, join with a sl st.
Sl st to center of snout.
Fasten off, leaving a length of yarn for forming snout.

BASE OF SNOUT
Row 1: Using A, ch3.
Row 2: 1sc in 2nd ch from hook (missed ch does not count as sc), 1sc in next ch. (*2 sts*)
Row 3: Ch1 (counts as first sc), 1sc in same sc, 1sc in next sc. (*3 sts*)
Row 4: Ch1, 1sc in same sc, 1sc in each sc to end. (*4 sts*)
Fasten off.
Trim off any excess fur.

EARS
(make 2)
Row 1: Using A, ch2.
Row 2: 1sc in 2nd ch from hook (missed ch does not count as sc). (*1 st*)
Row 3: Ch1 (counts as first sc), 1sc in same sc. (*2 sts*)
Row 4: Ch1, 1sc in same sc, 1sc in next sc. (*3 sts*)
Row 5: Ch1, 1sc in same sc, 1sc in each sc to end. (*4 sts*)
Row 6: Ch1, 1sc in same sc, 1sc in each sc to end. (*5 sts*)
Fasten off.

ARMS
(make 2)
Round 1: Using A, ch4, join with a sl st to form a ring.
Round 2: Ch1 (counts as first sc), 7sc in ring, join with a sl st. (*8 sts*)
Round 3: Ch1, 2sc in next sc, [1sc in next sc, 2sc in next sc] to end, join with a sl st. (*12 sts*)
Rounds 4–16: Ch1, 1sc in next sc, 1sc in each sc to end, join with a sl st.
Fasten off.

LEGS

(make 2)

Round 1: Using A, ch5, join with a sl st to form a ring.

Round 2: Ch1 (counts as first sc), 11sc in ring, join with a sl st. (*12 sts*)

Round 3: Ch1, 1sc in each of next 3 sc, [2sc in next sc] twice, 1sc in each of next 4 sc, [2sc in next sc] twice, join with a sl st. (*16 sts*)

Rounds 4-6: Ch1, 1sc in next sc, 1sc in each sc to end, join with a sl st.

Round 7: Ch1, 1sc in each of next 3 sc, [sc2tog] twice, 1sc in each of next 4 sc, [sc2tog] twice, join with a sl st. (*12 sts*)

Rounds 8-22: Ch1, 1sc in next sc, 1sc in each sc to end, join with a sl st.

Fasten off.

TAIL

Round 1: Using A, ch4, join with a sl st to form a ring.

Round 2: Ch1 (counts as first sc), 5sc in ring, join with a sl st. (*6 sts*)

Round 3: Ch1, 1sc in next sc, 1sc in each sc to end, join with a sl st.

Rep Row 3 until work measures 8in (20cm).

Fasten off.

SCARF

Row 1: Using B, ch8.

Row 2: 1hdc in 3rd ch from hook (missed 2 ch do not count as hdc), 1hdc in each ch to end. (*6 sts*)

Row 3: Ch2 (counts as first hdc), 1hdc in next hdc, 1hdc in each hdc to end.

Rep Row 3 until work measures 20in (50cm).

Fasten off.

TO MAKE UP

Add the safety eyes using the photo as a guide for positioning and secure with the backs (see page 141). Stuff the head firmly. Thread the yarn end onto a needle, gather the remaining sts together and fasten off.

To form the two puffed parts of the snout, stuff the snout lightly then wind the yarn end around the center and secure firmly at the back with a stitch. Using C, embroider the mouth markings onto the snout. Push the post of the safety nose through the crochet above the mouth markings and secure with the back. Sew the snout to the front of the face, then sew the base of snout below the snout. Use a yarn needle to insert lengths of C through the snout as whiskers. Trim to the length required and add a small amount of glue to hold in place. Sew the ears to the head using the photos as a guide for positioning.

Stuff the arms and sew them to the body. Stuff the legs and sew to the body in a sitting position.

Sew the tail to back of the body at the base.

Tie the scarf around the neck and hold in position with a couple of stitches.

SKILL RATING ● ○ ○

YARN AND MATERIALS
King Cole Glitz DK (97% acrylic, 3% polyester),
light worsted (DK) weight yarn, 317yd (290m)
per 3½oz (100g) ball
    Flame shade 3504
    Diamond White shade 483
    Silver shade 565
    Christmas shade 1698
    Pink shade 4721
    Christmas Green shade 3307
    Antique Gold shade 3503

King Cole Baby Glitz DK (97% acrylic,
5% polyester), light worsted (DK) weight
yarn, 317yd (290m) per 3½oz (100g) ball
    Sky shade 104

Small amount of black light worsted (DK) yarn

Toy fiberfill

HOOK AND EQUIPMENT
US G-6 (4mm) crochet hook
Yarn needle

FINISHED SIZE
Approx. 3in (7.5cm) tall

ABBREVIATIONS
See page 142.

PATTERN NOTE
Use your preferred color order
and combination.

colorful ball toys

With their soft filling, these pretty little cats will
charm any child. They are worked in single crochet
stitch throughout, and you can change the colors
and embroider any embellishments you like. Add
hanging loops to make them into perfect Christmas
tree decorations.

MAIN BALL

Round 1: Using color 1, ch4, join with a sl st to form a ring.
Round 2: Ch1 (counts as first sc), 7sc in ring, join with a sl st. (*8 sts*)
Round 3: Ch1, 1sc in same sc, 2sc in each sc to end, join with a sl st. (*16 sts*)
Round 4: Ch1, 2sc in next sc, [1sc in next sc, 2sc in next sc] to end, join with a sl st. (*24 sts*)
Round 5: Ch1, 1sc in next sc, 2sc in next sc, [1sc in each of next 2 sc, 2sc in next sc] to end, join with a sl st. (*32 sts*)
Round 6: Ch1, 1sc in each of next 2 sc, 2sc in next sc, [1sc in each of next 3 sc, 2sc in next sc] to end, join with a sl st. (*40 sts*)
Rounds 7–8: Ch1, 1sc in next sc, 1sc in each sc to end, join with a sl st.
Fasten off color 1, join in color 2.
Round 9: Ch1, 1scBLO in next sc, 1scBLO in each sc to end, join with a sl st.

Rounds 10–13: Ch1, 1sc in next sc, 1sc in each sc to end, join with a sl st.
Fasten off color 2, join in color 3.
Round 14: Ch1, 1scBLO in next sc, 1scBLO in each sc to end, join with a sl st.
Rounds 15 and 16: Ch1, 1sc in next sc, 1sc in each sc to end, join with a sl st.
Round 17: Ch1, 1sc in each of next 2 sc, sc2tog, [1sc in each of next 3 sc, sc2tog] to end, join with a sl st. (*32 sts*)
Round 18: Ch1, 1sc in next sc, sc2tog, [1sc in each of next 2 sc, sc2tog] to end, join with a sl st. (*24 sts*)
Round 19: Ch1, 1sc in next sc, 1sc in each sc to end, join with a sl st.
Round 20: Ch1, sc2tog, [1sc in next sc, sc2tog] to end, join with a sl st. (*16 sts*)
Stuff firmly.
Round 21: [Sc2tog] to end. (*8 sts*)
Add further stuffing if required.
Fasten off, leaving a length of yarn. Thread the yarn end onto a needle, gather remaining sts together, fasten off.

EARS
(make 2)
Row 1: Using any contrast color, ch2.
Row 2: 1sc in 2nd ch from hook (missed ch does not count as sc). (*1 st*)
Row 3: Ch1 (counts as first sc), 1sc in same sc. (*2 sts*)
Row 4: Ch1, 1sc in same sc, 1sc in next sc. (*3 sts*)
Row 5: Ch1, 1sc in same sc, 1sc in each sc to end. (*4 sts*)
Fasten off.

FAN
Row 1: Using any contrast color, ch4.
Row 2: 7dc in 4th ch from hook.
Fasten off.

TO MAKE UP
Sew on the fan at center front, just above first change of color. Embroider the mouth, face markings and whiskers in straight stitches using any colors, and add the nose in satin stitch (see page 141). Sew the ears to the top of the head.

Add a loop of yarn at the top to produce a hanging cat for a Christmas tree decoration (optional).

Bring luck and happiness into your home with this pretty little Japanese lucky cat. Crocheted in simple single crochet stitch throughout, it would make a perfect gift for friends and family.

japanese lucky cat

SKILL RATING ● ● ○

YARN AND MATERIALS
King Cole Glitz DK (97% acrylic, 3% polyester), light worsted (DK) weight yarn, 317yd (290m) per 3½oz (100g) ball
    ½ ball of Diamond White shade 483 (A)
    Small amounts of:
    Flame shade 3504 (B)
    Antique Gold shade 3503 (C)

Small amount of black light worsted (DK) weight yarn (D)

Small amount of pink light worsted (DK) weight yarn (E)

Pair of 15mm cat safety eyes

Toy fiberfill

HOOK AND EQUIPMENT
US G-6 (4mm) crochet hook

Yarn needle

FINISHED SIZE
Height 8in (20cm)

ABBREVIATIONS
See page 142.

PATTERN NOTE
If giving the cat to a young child, substitute the safety eyes and nose with embroidery in yarn (see page 141).

HEAD AND BODY
Round 1: Using A, ch4, join with a sl st to form a ring.
Round 2: Ch1 (counts as first sc), 7sc in ring, join with a sl st. (*8 sts*)
Round 3: Ch1, 1sc in same sc, 2sc in each sc to end, join with a sl st. (*16 sts*)
Round 4: Ch1, 2sc in next sc, [1sc in next sc, 2sc in next sc] to end, join with a sl st. (*24 sts*)
Round 5: Ch1, 1sc in next sc, 2sc in next sc, [1sc in each of next 2 sc, 2sc in next sc] to end, join with a sl st. (*32 sts*)
Round 6: Ch1, 1sc in next sc, 1sc in each sc to end, join with a sl st.
Round 7: Ch1, 1sc in each of next 2 sc, 2sc in next sc, [1sc in each of next 3 sc, 2sc in next sc] to end, join with a sl st. (*40 sts*)
Rounds 8–13: Ch1, 1sc in next sc, 1sc in each sc to end, join with a sl st.
Round 14: Ch1, 1sc in each of next 2 sc, sc2tog, [1sc in each of next 3 sc, sc2tog] to end, join with a sl st. (*32 sts*)
Round 15: Ch1, 1sc in next sc, sc2tog, [1sc in each of next 2 sc, sc2tog] to end, join with a sl st. (*24 sts*)
Round 16: Ch1, 1sc in next sc, 1sc in each sc to end, join with a sl st.
Attach safety eyes, using photograph as a guide for positioning, and secure with backs (see page 141). Stuff head.
Round 17: Ch1, 1sc in next sc, 2sc in next sc, [1sc in each of next 2 sc, 2sc in next sc] to end, join with a sl st. (*32 sts*)
Round 18: Ch1, 1sc in each of next 2 sc, 2sc in next sc, [1sc in each of next 3 sc, 2sc in next sc] to end, join with a sl st. (*40 sts*)
Round 19: Ch1, 1sc in each of next 3 sc, 2sc in next sc, [1sc in each of next 4 sc, 2sc in next sc] to end, join with a sl st. (*48 sts*)
Rounds 20–29: Ch1, 1sc in next sc, 1sc in each sc to end, join with a sl st.
Round 30: Ch1, 1sc in each of next 3 sc, sc2tog, [1sc in each of next 4 sc, sc2tog] to end, join with a sl st. (*40 sts*)

Round 31: Ch1, 1sc in each of next 2 sc, sc2tog, [1sc in each of next 3 sc, sc2tog] to end, join with a sl st. (*32 sts*)
Round 32: Ch1, 1sc in next sc, sc2tog, [1sc in each of next 2 sc, sc2tog] to end, join with a sl st. (*24 sts*)
Round 33: Ch1, sc2tog, [1sc in next sc, sc2tog] to end, join with a sl st. (*16 sts*)
Round 34: Ch1, 1sc in next sc, sc2tog, [1sc in each of next 2 sc, sc2tog] to end, join with a sl st. (*12 sts*)
Fasten off, leaving a length of yarn.

SNOUT
Round 1: Using A, ch4, join with a sl st to form a ring.
Round 2: Ch1 (counts as first sc), 7sc in ring, join with a sl st. (*8 sts*)
Round 3: Ch1, 1sc in same sc, 2sc in next sc, 1sc in each of next 2 sc, 2sc in each of next 2 sc, 1sc in each of next 2 sc to end, join with a sl st. (*12 sts*)
Round 4: Ch1, 1sc in next sc, 1sc in each sc to end, join with a sl st.
Fasten off.

INNER EARS
(make 2)
Row 1: Using B, ch2.
Row 2: 1sc in 2nd ch from hook (missed ch does not count as sc). (*1 st*)
Row 3: Ch1 (counts as first sc), 1sc in same sc. (*2 sts*)
Row 4: Ch1, 1sc in same sc, 1sc in next sc. (*3 sts*)
Row 5: Ch1, 1sc in same sc, 1sc in each sc to end. (*4 sts*)
Row 6: Ch1, 1sc in same sc, 1sc in each sc to end. (*5 sts*)
Fasten off.

OUTER EARS
(make 2)
Row 1: Using A, ch2.
Row 2: 1sc in 2nd ch from hook (missed ch does not count as sc). (*1 st*)
Row 3: Ch1 (counts as first sc), 1sc in same sc. (*2 sts*)
Row 4: Ch1, 1sc in same sc, 1sc in next sc. (*3 sts*)
Row 5: Ch1, 1sc in same sc, 1sc in each sc to end. (*4 sts*)
Row 6: Ch1, 1sc in same sc, 1sc in each sc to end. (*5 sts*)
Fasten off.

ARMS

(make 2)

Round 1: Using A, ch5, join with a sl st to form a ring.

Round 2: Ch1 (counts as first sc), 9sc in ring, join with a sl st. (*10 sts*)

Rounds 3–12: Ch1, 1sc in next sc, 1sc in each sc to end, join with a sl st.

Fasten off.

THIGHS

(make 2)

Round 1: Using A, ch4, join with a sl st to form a ring.

Round 2: Ch1 (counts as first sc), 7sc in ring, join with a sl st. (*8 sts*)

Round 3: Ch1, 1sc in same sc, 2sc in each sc to end, join with a sl st. (*16 sts*)

Round 4: Ch1, 2sc in next sc, [1sc in next sc, 2sc in next sc] to end, join with a sl st. (*24 sts*)

Round 5: Ch1, 1sc in next sc, 1sc in each sc to end, join with a sl st.

Fasten off.

FEET

(make 2)

Round 1: Using A, ch5, join with a sl st to form a ring.

Round 2: Ch1 (counts as first sc), 9sc in ring, join with a sl st. (*10 sts*)

Rounds 3–5: Ch1, 1sc in next sc, 1sc in each sc to end, join with a sl st.

Round 6: Ch1, 2sc in next sc, [1sc in next sc, 2sc in next sc] to end, join with a sl st. (*15 sts*)

Fasten off.

COLLAR

Row 1: Using B, ch36.

Row 2: 1sc in 2nd ch from hook (missed ch does not count as sc), 1sc in each ch to end. (*35 sts*)

Row 3: Ch1 (counts as first sc), 1sc in next sc, 1sc in each sc to end.

Fasten off.

KOBAN COIN

Round 1: Using C, ch5.

Round 2: 1sc in 2nd ch from hook (missed ch does not count as sc), 1sc in each ch to last ch, 3sc in last ch, working along bottom of chain, 1sc in each ch to end, 1sc in end of row, join with a sl st. (*10 sts*)

Rounds 3–7: Ch1 (counts as first sc), 1sc in next sc, 1sc in each sc to end, join with a sl st.

Fasten off.

TO MAKE UP

Stuff body firmly. Thread the length of yarn onto a needle, gather the remaining stitches together to close the gap and fasten off.

Using E and B, embroider the nose and mouth markings on the snout. Stuff lightly and sew the snout to the head.

Using D, embroider a thin line around each eye using the photograph as a reference. Using D, embroider the whiskers on the face in straight stitch (see page 141).

Place an inner ear on top of an outer ear and, using A, work two rounds of single crochet through both layers to join, working 2sc into each corner stitch. Sew the ears on top of the head, using the photo as a guide for positioning.

Sew the collar in place around the neck and use C to embroider a gold button at the center front.

Stuff the arms and thighs and sew to the body, using the photo as a guide for positioning.

Stuff the feet and sew to the body at the end of the thighs.

Using D, embroider the markings on the coin. Sew the coin into position using the photograph as a guide.

Using B, embroider the claws on the arms and feet.

What a great companion for a child to cuddle. Crocheted in very soft yarn in single crochet stitch, this is a great project for the confident beginner. Lawrence would also make a lovely gift for adults, too.

lawrence the cuddly lion

SKILL RATING ● ● ○

YARN AND MATERIALS
King Cole Big Value Super Chunky (100% acrylic), super bulky (super chunky) weight yarn, 90yd (81m) per 3½oz (100g) ball
   3 balls of Brass shade 3400 (A)
   ½ ball of Brown shade 31 (B)
   Small amount of White shade 1758 (C)
Small amount of black bulky (chunky) weight yarn (D)

Pair of 24mm safety eyes

Toy fiberfill

HOOK AND EQUIPMENT
US J-10 (6mm) crochet hook

Yarn needle

Stiff brush or pet brush

Hairspray (optional)

FINISHED SIZE
Approx. 20in (51cm) standing

ABBREVIATIONS
See page 142.

PATTERN NOTE
If giving the cat to a young child, substitute the safety eyes and nose with embroidery in yarn (see page 141).

BODY
Round 1: Using A, ch5, join with a sl st to form a ring.
Round 2: Ch1 (counts as first sc), 11sc in ring, join with a sl st. (*12 sts*)
Round 3: Ch1, [2sc in next sc] twice, 1sc in each of next 4 sc, [2sc in next sc] twice, 1sc in each of next 3 sc, join with a sl st. (*16 sts*)
Round 4: Ch1, 1sc in next sc, 1sc in each sc to end, join with a sl st.
Round 5: Ch1, 2sc in next sc, [1sc in next sc, 2sc in next sc] to end, join with a sl st. (*24 sts*)
Round 6: Ch1, 1sc in next sc, 1sc in each sc to end, join with a sl st.
Round 7: Ch1, 1sc in next sc, 2sc in next sc, [1sc in each of next 2 sc, 2sc in next sc] to end, join with a sl st. (*32 sts*)
Rounds 8 and 9: Ch1, 1sc in next sc, 1sc in each sc to end. join with a sl st.
Round 10: Ch1, 1sc in each of next 2 sc, 2sc in next sc, [1sc in each of next 3 sc, 2sc in next sc] to end, join with a sl st. (*40 sts*)
Rounds 11–20: Ch1, 1sc in next sc, 1sc in each sc to end, join with a sl st.
Round 21: Ch1, 1sc in each of next 2 sc, sc2tog, [1sc in each of next 3 sc, sc2tog] to end, join with a sl st. (*32 sts*)
Round 22: Ch1, 1sc in next sc, 1sc in each sc to end, join with a sl st.
Round 23: Ch1, 1sc in next sc, sc2tog, [1sc in each of next 2 sc, sc2tog] to end, join with a sl st. (*24 sts*)
Round 24: Ch1, 1sc in next sc, 1sc in each sc to end, join with a sl st. Stuff body firmly.
Round 25: [Sc2tog] to end, join with a sl st. (*12 sts*)
Fasten off, leaving a length of yarn. Thread yarn end onto needle, gather remaining sts together, fasten off.

HEAD

Round 1: Using A, ch5, join with a sl st to form a ring.
Round 2: Ch1 (counts as first sc), 9sc in ring, join with a sl st. (*10 sts*)
Round 3: Ch1, 1sc in same sc, 2sc in each sc to end, join with a sl st. (*20 sts*)
Round 4: Ch1, 2sc in next sc, [1sc in next sc, 2sc in next sc] to end, join with a sl st. (*30 sts*)
Rounds 5 and 6: Ch1, 1sc in next sc, 1sc in each sc to end, join with a sl st.
Round 7: Ch1, 1sc in each of next 3 sc, 2sc in next sc, [1sc in each of next 4 sc, 2sc in next sc] to end, join with a sl st. (*36 sts*)
Rounds 8–13: Ch1, 1sc in next sc, 1sc in each sc to end, join with a sl st.
Round 14: Ch1, 1sc in each of next 3 sc, sc2tog, [1sc in each of next 4 sc, sc2tog] to end, join with a sl st. (*30 sts*)
Round 15: Ch1, 1sc in each of next 2 sc, sc2tog, [1sc in each of next 3 sc, sc2tog] to end, join with a sl st. (*24 sts*)
Round 16: Ch1, 1sc in next sc, 1sc in each sc to end, join with a sl st.
Round 17: [Sc2tog] to end, join with a sl st. (*12 sts*)
Fasten off.

SNOUT

Round 1: Using A, ch4, join with a sl st to form a ring.
Round 2: Ch1 (counts as first sc), 7sc in ring, join with a sl st. (*8 sts*)
Round 3: Ch1, 1sc in same sc, 2sc in each sc to end, join with a sl st. (*16 sts*)
Rounds 4–7: Ch1, 1sc in next sc, 1sc in each sc to end, join with a sl st.
Fasten off.

EARS

(make 2)
Round 1: Using A, ch4, join with a sl st to form a ring.
Round 2: Ch1 (counts as first sc), 7sc in ring, join with a sl st. (*8 sts*)
Round 3: Ch1, 2sc in next sc, [1sc in next sc, 2sc in next sc] to end, join with sl st. (*12 sts*)
Rounds 4–6: Ch1, 1sc in next sc, 1sc in each sc to end, join with a sl st.
Fasten off.

ARMS

(make 2)
Round 1: Using A, ch4, join with a sl st to form a ring.
Round 2: Ch1 (counts as first sc), 7sc in ring, join with a sl st. (*8 sts*)
Round 3: Ch1, 2sc in next sc, [1sc in next sc, 2sc in next sc] to end join with sl st. (*12 sts*)
Round 4: Ch1, 1sc in next sc, 1sc in each sc to end, join with sl st.
Round 5: Ch1, 2sc in next sc, [1sc in next sc, 2sc in next sc] to end, join with sl st. (*18 sts*)
Rounds 6 and 7: Ch1, 1sc in next sc, 1sc in each sc to end, join with a sl st.
Round 8: Ch1, sc2tog, [1sc in next sc, sc2tog] to end, join with a sl st. (*12 sts*)
Rounds 9–20: Ch1, 1sc in next sc, 1sc in each sc to end, join with a sl st.
Fasten off.

LEGS

(make 2)
Round 1: Using A, ch5, join with a sl st to form a ring.
Round 2: Ch1 (counts as first sc), 9sc in ring, join with a sl st. (*10 sts*)
Round 3: Ch1, 1sc in each of next 2 sc, [2sc in next sc] twice, 1sc in each of next 3 sc, [2sc in next sc] twice, join with a sl st. (*14 sts*)
Round 4: Ch1, 1sc in each of next 4 sc, [2sc in next sc] twice, 1sc in each of next 5 sc, [2sc in next sc] twice, join with a sl st. (*18 sts*)

Round 5: Ch1, 1sc in each of next 6 sc, [2sc in next sc] twice, 1sc in each of next 7 sc, [2sc in next sc] twice, join with a sl st. (*22 sts*)
Rounds 6 and 7: Ch1, 1sc in next sc, 1sc in each sc to end, join with a sl st.
Round 8: Ch1, sc2tog, [1sc in next sc, sc2tog] 3 times, 1sc in each sc to end, join with a sl st. (*18 sts*)
Round 9: Ch1, sc2tog, [1sc in next sc, sc2tog] twice, 1sc in each sc to end, join with a sl st. (*15 sts*)
Rounds 10–20: Ch1, 1sc in next sc, 1sc in each sc to end, join with a sl st.
Fasten off.

TAIL
Round 1: Using A, ch4, join with a sl st to form a ring.
Round 2: Ch1 (counts as first sc), 7sc in ring, join with a sl st. (*8 sts*)
Round 3: Ch1, 1sc in next sc, 1sc in each sc to end.
Rep Round 3 until work measures approx. 8in (20cm).
Fasten off.

TO MAKE UP
Using D, embroider markings for the nose and mouth onto the snout. Stuff and sew the snout to the head. Add the safety eyes using the photo as a guide for positioning and secure with the backs (see page 141). Using D, embroider curved eyebrows over the eyes with straight stitches (see page 141).

Stuff the head until firm. Thread the yarn end into a needle and gather the remaining stitches, then pull tightly together. Fasten off. Sew the ears to the head, using the photo as a guide for positioning.

Sew the head to the body.

Stuff the arms and legs and sew to the body. Using D, embroider claws on each paw. Sew the tail to the back of the body.

Adding the mane and tail end
Cut lengths of B approx. 6in (15cm) long.

Take two lengths at a time and, with the crochet hook, work a round of fringe all around the face (see page 141). Continue adding the fringe over the top of the head and to cover the back of the head. Trim and brush if required.

Add some fringe to the base of tail. Brush for the fluffy effect and trim to length required.

Cut a few short few lengths of C and add these under the chin to the end of the snout. Brush and trim to length.

techniques

This section guides you through all the crochet and finishing techniques that you will need to make the projects in this book.

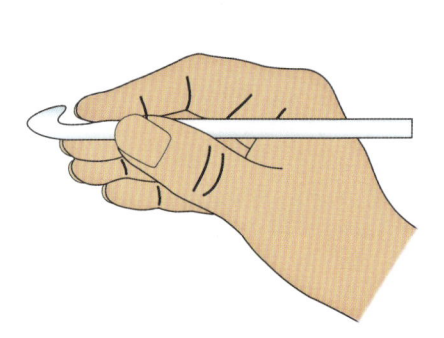

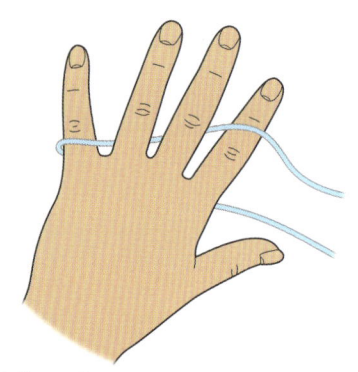

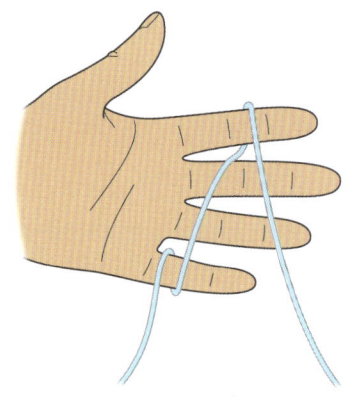

Holding the hook

Pick up your hook as though you are picking up a pen or pencil. Keeping the hook held loosely between your fingers and thumb, turn your hand so that the palm is facing up and the hook is balanced in your hand and resting in the space between your index finger and your thumb.

You can also hold the hook like a knife—this may be easier if you are working with a large hook or with bulky (chunky) yarn. Choose the method that you find most comfortable.

Holding the yarn

1 Pick up the yarn with your little finger in the opposite hand to your hook, with your palm facing upward and with the short end in front. Turn your hand to face downward, with the yarn on top of your index finger and under the other two fingers and wrapped right around the little finger, as shown above.

2 Turn your hand to face you, ready to hold the work in your middle finger and thumb. Keeping your index finger only at a slight curve, hold the work or the slip knot using the same hand, between your middle finger and your thumb and just below the crochet hook and loop/s on the hook.

Holding the hook and yarn while crocheting

Keep your index finger, with the yarn draped over it, at a slight curve, and hold your work (or the slip knot) using the same hand, between your middle finger and your thumb and just below the crochet hook and loop/s on the hook.

As you draw the loop through the hook release the yarn on the index finger to allow the loop to stay loose on the hook. If you tense your index finger, the yarn will become too tight and pull the loop on the hook too tight for you to draw the yarn through.

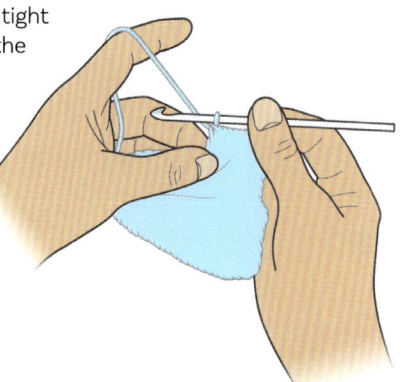

Holding the hook and yarn for left-handers

Some left-handers learn to crochet like right-handers, but others learn with everything reversed—with the hook in the left hand and the yarn in the right.

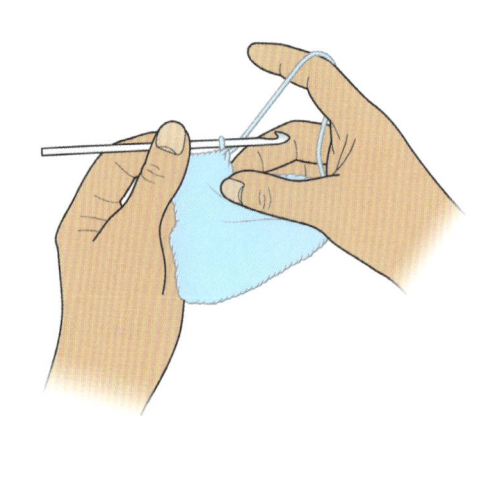

Making a slip knot

The simplest way is to make a circle with the yarn, so that the loop is facing downward.

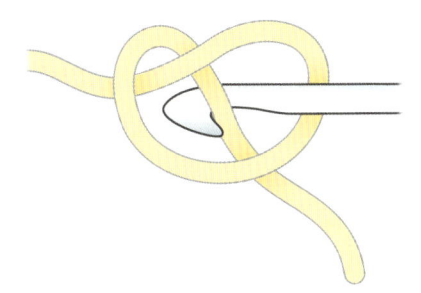 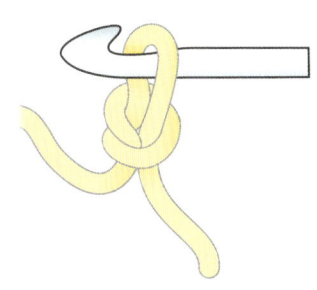

1 In one hand hold the circle at the top where the yarn crosses, and let the tail drop down at the back so that it falls across the center of the loop. With your free hand or the tip of a crochet hook, pull a loop through the circle.

2 Put the hook into the loop and pull gently so that it forms a loose loop on the hook.

Yarn over hook (yoh)

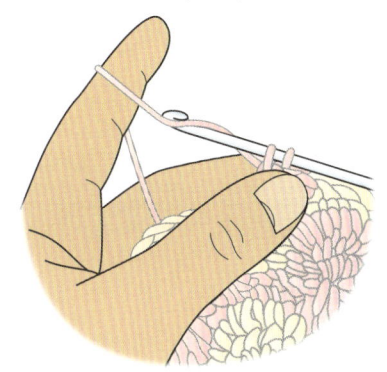

To create a stitch, catch the yarn from behind with the hook pointing upward. As you gently pull the yarn through the loop on the hook, turn the hook so it faces downward and slide the yarn through the loop. The loop on the hook should be kept loose enough for the hook to slide through easily.

Chain (ch)

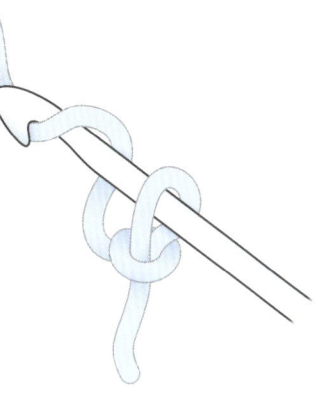 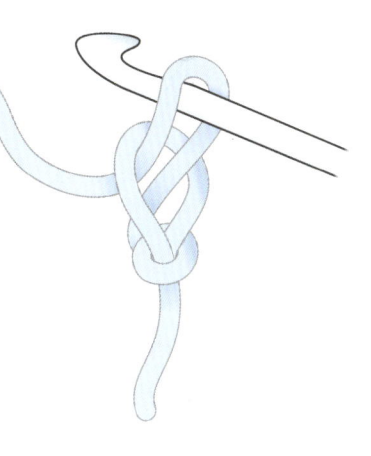

1 Using the hook, wrap the yarn over the hook ready to pull it through the loop on the hook.

2 Pull through, creating a new loop on the hook. Continue in this way to create a chain of the required length.

Chain ring

If you are crocheting a round shape, one way of starting off is by crocheting a number of chains following the instructions in your pattern, and then joining them into a circle.

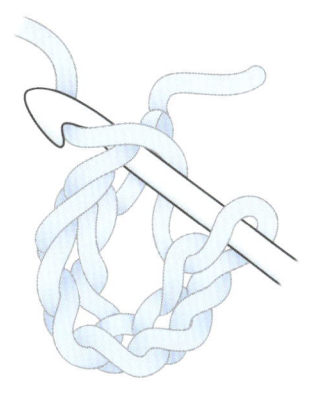 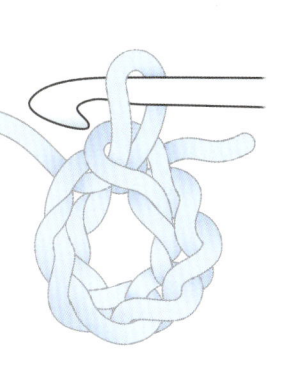

1 To join the chain into a circle, insert the crochet hook into the first chain that you made (not into the slip knot), yarn over hook.

2 Pull the yarn through the chain and through the loop on your hook at the same time, thereby creating a slip stitch and forming a circle. You now have a chain ring ready to work stitches into as instructed in the pattern.

Magic ring

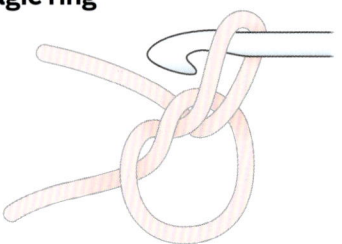

This is a useful starting technique if you do not want a visible hole in the center of your round. Loop the yarn around your finger, insert the hook through the ring, yarn over hook, pull through the ring to make the first chain. Work the number of stitches required into the ring and then pull the end to tighten the center ring and close the hole.

Slip stitch (sl st)

A slip stitch doesn't create any height and is often used as the last stitch to create a smooth and even round or row.

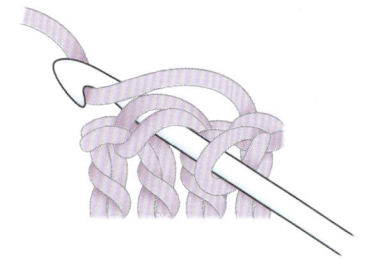

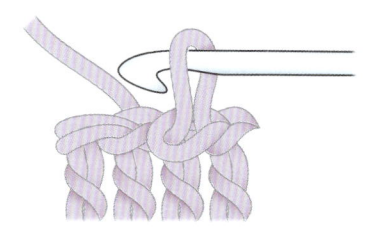

1 To make a slip stitch: first put the hook through the work, yarn over hook.

2 Pull the yarn through both the work and through the loop on the hook at the same time, so you will have 1 loop on the hook.

Making rounds

When working in rounds the work is not turned, so you are always working from one side. Depending on the pattern you are working, a "round" can be square. Start each round by making one or more chains to create the height you need for the stitch you are working:

Single crochet = 1 chain
Half double crochet = 2 chains
Double crochet = 3 chains
Treble crochet = 4 chains

Work the required stitches to complete the round. At the end of the round, slip stitch into the top of the chain to close the round.

Continuous spiral

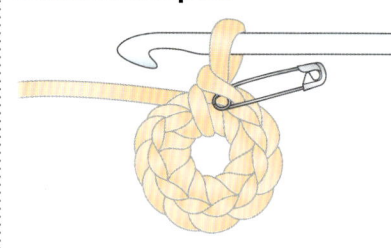

If you work in a spiral you do not need a turning chain. After completing the base ring, place a stitch marker in the first stitch and then continue to crochet around. When you have made a round and reached the point where the stitch marker is, work this stitch, take out the stitch marker from the previous round and put it back into the first stitch of the new round. A safety pin or piece of yarn in a contrasting color makes a good stitch marker.

Making rows

When making straight rows you turn the work at the end of each row and make a turning chain to create the height you need for the stitch you are working with, as for making rounds.

Single crochet = 1 chain
Half double crochet = 2 chains
Double crochet = 3 chains
Treble crochet = 4 chains

Working into top of stitch

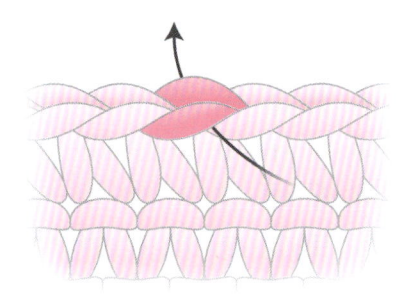

Unless otherwise directed, always insert the hook under both of the two loops on top of the stitch—this is the standard technique.

Working into front loop of stitch (FLO)

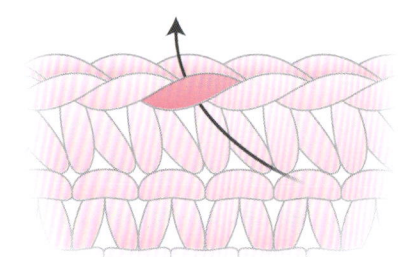

To work into the front loop of a stitch, pick up the front loop from underneath at the front of the work.

Working into back loop of stitch (BLO)

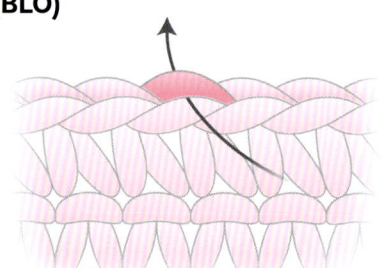

To work into the back loop of the stitch, insert the hook between the front and the back loop, picking up the back loop from the front of the work.

Single crochet (sc)

 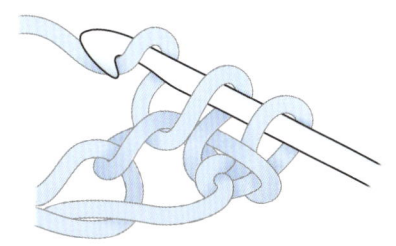

1 Insert the hook into your work, yarn over hook and pull the yarn through the work only. You will then have 2 loops on the hook.

2 Yarn over hook again and pull through the 2 loops on the hook. You will then have 1 loop on the hook.

Half double crochet (hdc)

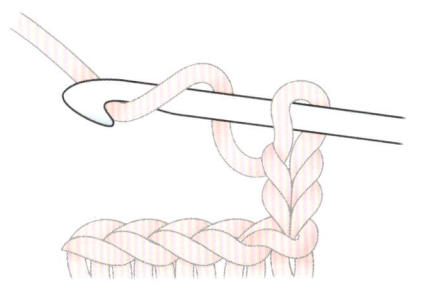 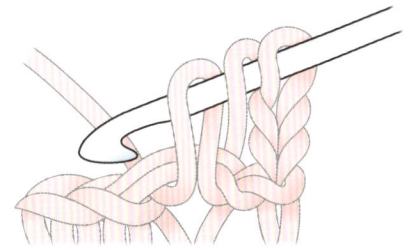 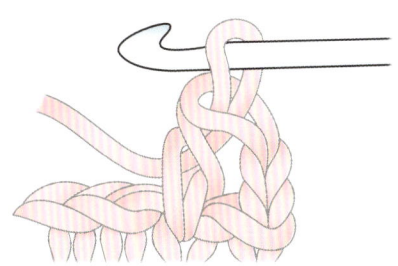

1 Before inserting the hook into the work, wrap the yarn over the hook and put the hook through the work with the yarn wrapped around.

2 Yarn over hook again and pull through the first loop on the hook. You now have 3 loops on the hook.

3 Yarn over hook and pull the yarn through all 3 loops. You will be left with 1 loop on the hook.

Double crochet (dc)

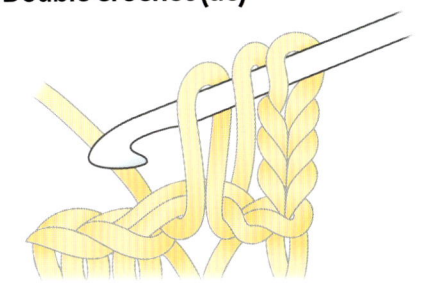  

1 Before inserting the hook into the work, wrap the yarn over the hook. Put the hook through the work with the yarn wrapped around, yarn over hook again and pull through the stitch. You now have 3 loops on the hook.

2 Yarn over hook again, pull the yarn through the first 2 loops on the hook. You now have 2 loops on the hook.

3 Pull the yarn through 2 loops again. You will be left with 1 loop on the hook.

Treble crochet (tr)

Yarn over hook twice, insert the hook into the stitch, yarn over hook, pull a loop through (4 loops on hook), yarn over hook, pull the yarn through 2 loops (3 loops on hook), yarn over hook, pull a loop through the next 2 loops (2 loops on hook), yarn over hook, pull a loop through the last 2 loops. You will be left with 1 loop on the hook.

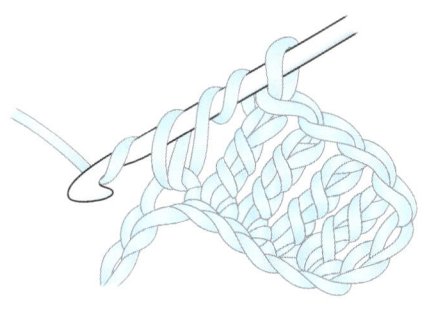

Working around the front or back post

Stitches can also be worked around the "posts"—or "stems"—of the stitches in the previous row/round. These steps show how to work a double crochet around the front and the back of the post, but the same principle applies to other stitches worked around the post. They can be used to create texture.

Raised double crochet round front

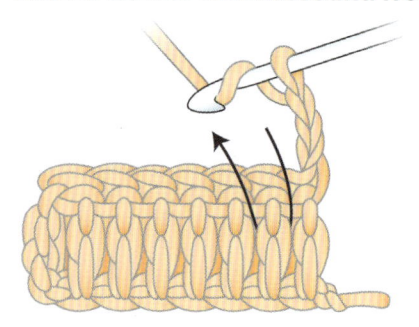 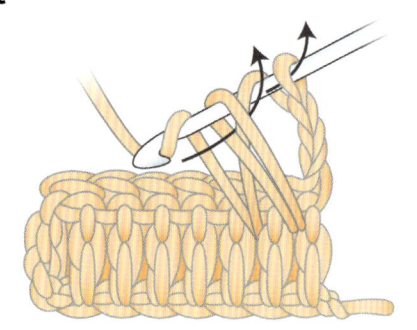 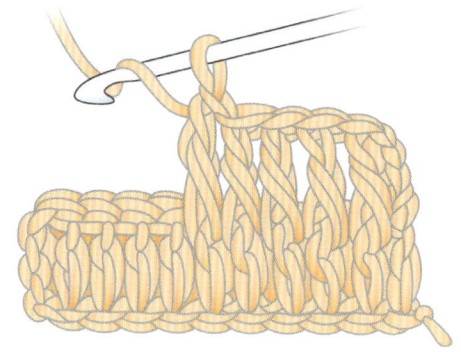

1 Yarn over hook and insert the hook from the front and around the post (the stem) of the next double crochet from right to left.

2 Yarn over hook and pull the yarn through the work, yarn over hook and pull the yarn through the first 2 loops on the hook.

3 Yarn over hook and pull the yarn through the 2 loops on the hook (1 loop on the hook).

Raised double crochet round back

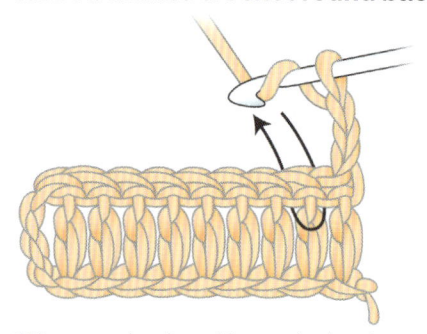 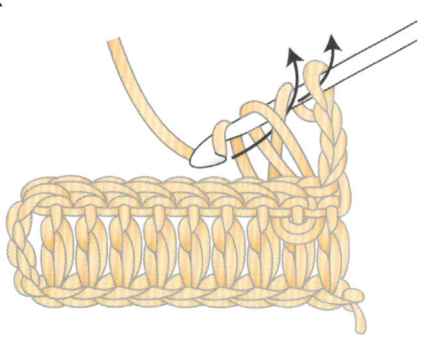 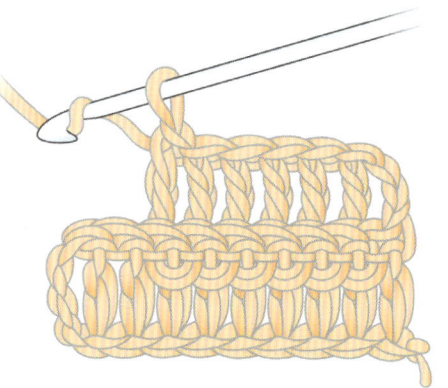

1 Yarn over hook and insert the hook from the back and around the post (the stem) of the next double crochet as directed in the pattern from right to left.

2 Yarn over hook and pull the yarn through the work, yarn over hook and pull the yarn through the first 2 loops on the hook.

3 Yarn over hook and pull the yarn through the 2 loops on the hook (1 loop on the hook).

Spike stitch

This stitch is also sometimes called elongated or long single crochet. You just work an ordinary single crochet stitch, but into the stitch that's one, two or more rows below, which creates a "V" of yarn on the surface. These instructions are for an spike stitch worked into the top of the stitch two rows below.

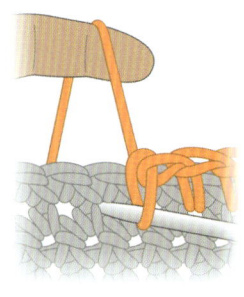 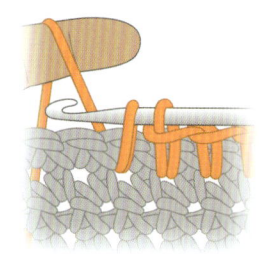 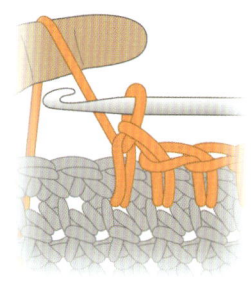

1 Using a contrast yarn, insert your hook into the space one row below the next stitch—this is the top of the stitch two rows below, so the same place that the stitch in the previous row is worked.

2 Yarn round hook and draw a loop up so it's level with the original loop on your hook.

3 Yarn over hook and pull through both loops to complete the elongated single crochet.

Increasing

Make two or three stitches into one stitch or space from the previous row. The illustration shows a double crochet increase being made.

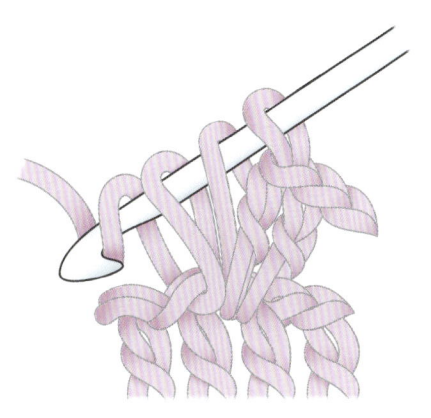

Decreasing

You can decrease by either missing the next stitch and continuing to crochet, or by crocheting two or more stitches together. The basic technique for crocheting stitches together is the same, no matter which stitch you are using. The following example shows sc2tog.

Single crochet two stitches together (sc2tog)

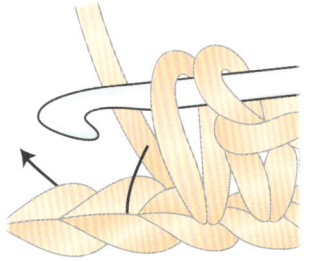 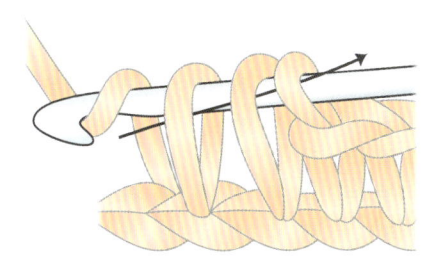

1 Insert the hook into your work, yarn over hook and pull the yarn through the work (2 loops on hook). Insert the hook in next stitch, yarn over hook and pull the yarn through.

2 Yarn over hook again and pull through all 3 loops on the hook. You will then have 1 loop on the hook.

Joining yarn at the end of a row or round

You can use this technique when changing color, or when joining in a new ball of yarn as one runs out.

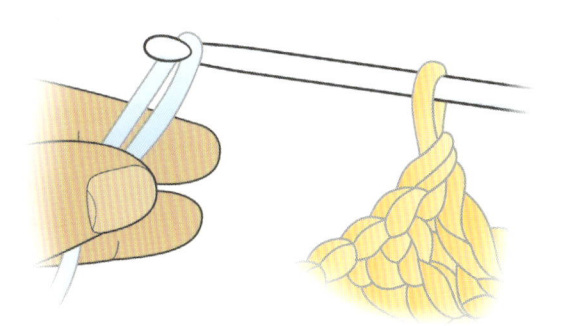 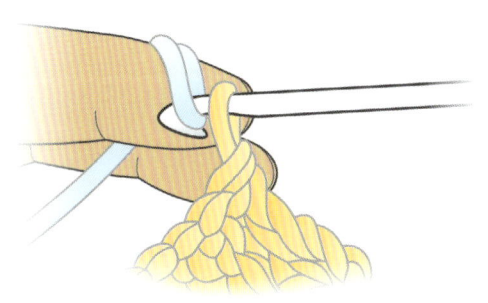

1 Keep the loop of the old yarn on the hook. Drop the tail and catch a loop of the new yarn with the crochet hook.

2 Draw the new yarn through the loop on the hook, keeping the old loop drawn tight and continue as instructed in the pattern.

Joining in new yarn after fastening off

1 Fasten off the old color (see opposite). Make a slip knot with the new color (see page 133). Insert the hook into the stitch at the beginning of the next row, then through the slip knot.

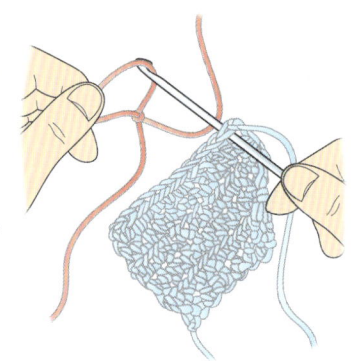

2 Draw the loop of the slip knot through to the front of the work. Carry on working using the new color, following the instructions in the pattern.

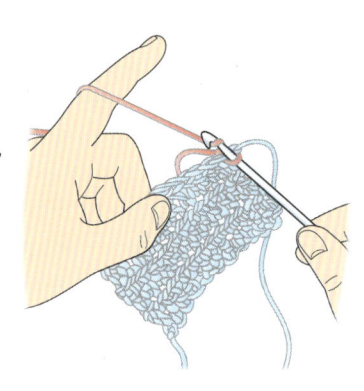

Joining yarn in the middle of a row or round

For a neat color join in the middle of a row or round, use these methods.

Joining a new color into single crochet

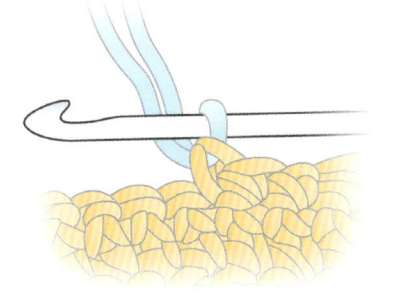
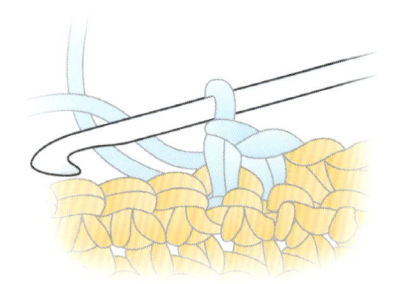

1 Make a single crochet stitch (see page 135), but do not draw the final loop through, so there are 2 loops on the hook. Drop the old yarn, catch the new yarn with the hook and draw it through both loops to complete the stitch and join in the new color at the same time.

2 Continue to crochet with the new yarn. Cut the old yarn leaving a 6in (15cm) tail and weave the tail in (see right) after working a row, or once the work is complete.

Joining a new color into double crochet

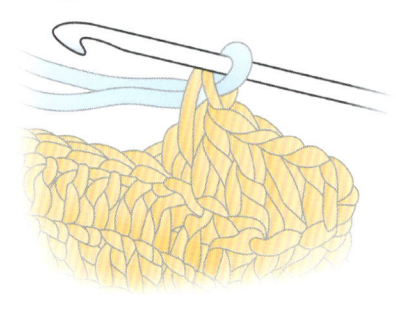
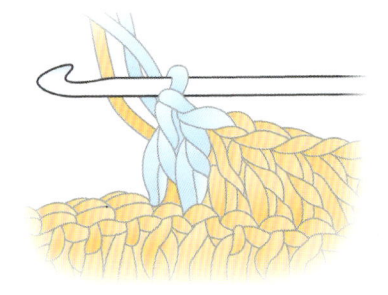

1 Make a double crochet stitch (see page 135), but do not draw the final loop through, so there are 2 loops on the hook. Drop the old yarn, catch the new yarn with the hook and draw it through both loops to complete the stitch and join in the new color at the same time.

2 Continue to crochet with the new yarn. Cut the old yarn leaving a 6in (15cm) tail and weave the tail in (see right) after working a row, or once the work is complete.

Enclosing a yarn tail

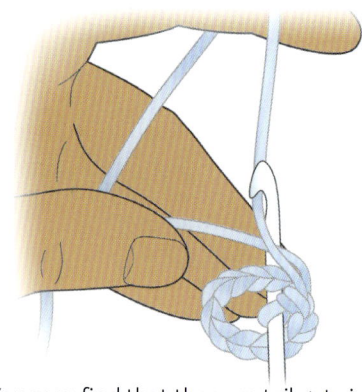

You may find that the yarn tail gets in the way as you work; you can enclose this into the stitches as you go by placing the tail at the back as you wrap the yarn. This also saves having to sew this tail end in later.

Fastening off

When you have finished crocheting, you need to fasten off the stitches to stop all your work unraveling.

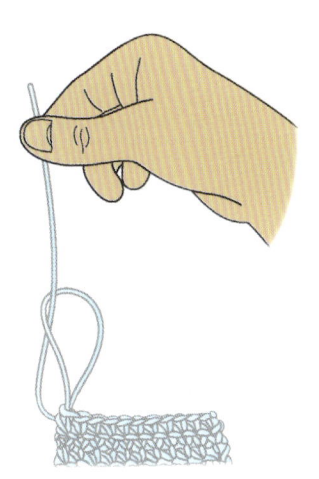

Draw up the final loop of the last stitch to make it bigger. Cut the yarn, leaving a tail of approximately 4in (10cm)—unless a longer end is needed for sewing up. Pull the tail all the way through the loop and pull the loop up tightly.

Sewing in yarn ends

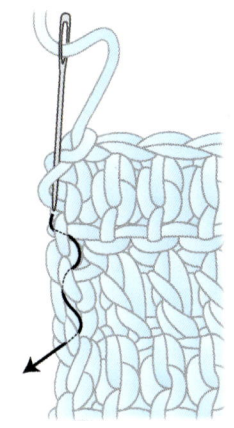

It is important to sew in the tail ends of the yarn so that they are secure and your crochet won't unravel. Thread a yarn needle with the tail end of yarn. On the wrong side, take the needle through the crochet one stitch down on the edge, then take it through the stitches, working in a gentle zigzag. Work through four or five stitches then return in the opposite direction. Remove the needle, pull the crochet gently to stretch it and trim the end.

Blocking

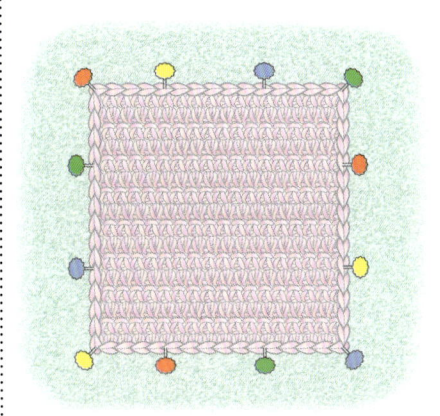

Crochet can tend to curl, so to make flat pieces stay flat you may need to block them. Pin the piece out to the correct size and shape on an ironing board or some soft foam mats (such as the ones sold as children's play mats). Spray the crochet with water and leave it to dry completely before unpinning and removing from the board or mats.

Making an oversewn seam

An oversewn join gives a nice flat seam and is the simplest and most common joining technique.

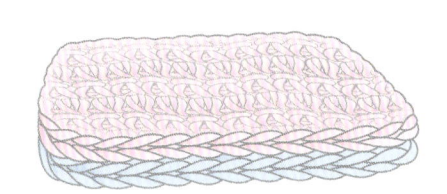

1 Thread a yarn needle with the yarn you're using in the project. Place the pieces to be joined with right sides together (unless the pattern says otherwise).

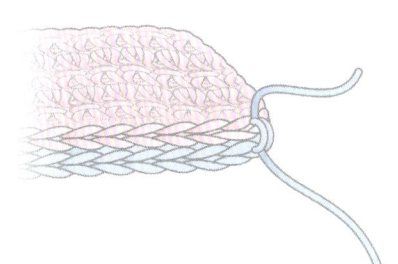

2 Insert the needle in one corner in the top loops of the stitches of both pieces and pull up the yarn, leaving a tail of about 2in (5cm). Go into the same place with the needle and pull up the yarn again; repeat two or three times to secure the yarn at the start of the seam.

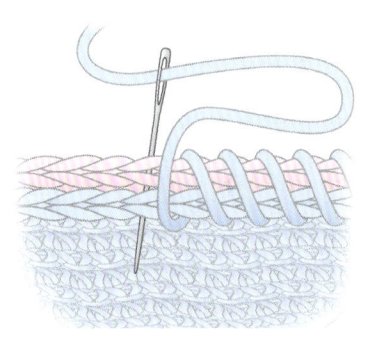

3 Join the pieces together by taking the needle through the loops at the top of corresponding stitches on each piece to the end. Fasten off the yarn at the end, as in step 2.

Making a single crochet seam or slip stitch seam

With a single crochet seam you join two pieces together using a crochet hook and working a single crochet stitch through both pieces, instead of sewing them together with a tail of yarn and a yarn needle. This makes a quick and strong seam and gives a slightly raised finish to the edging. For a less raised seam, follow the same basic technique, but work each stitch in slip stitch rather than single crochet.

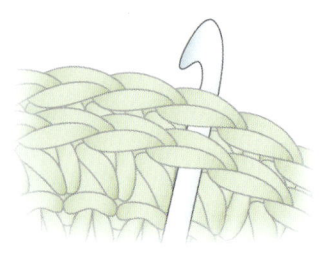

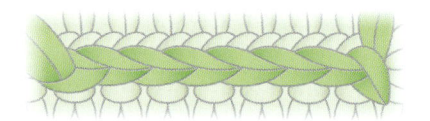

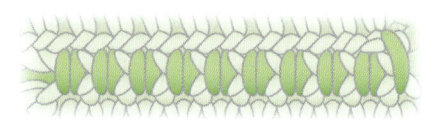

1 Start by lining up the two pieces with wrong sides together. Insert the hook in the top 2 loops of the stitch of the first piece, then into the corresponding stitch on the second piece.

2 Complete the single crochet stitch as normal and continue on the next stitches as directed in the pattern. This gives a raised effect if the single crochet stitches are made on the right side of the work.

3 You can work with the wrong side of the work facing (with the pieces right side facing) if you don't want this effect and it still creates a good strong join.

Surface crochet

Surface crochet is a simple way to add extra decoration to a finished item, working slip stitches over the surface of the fabric.

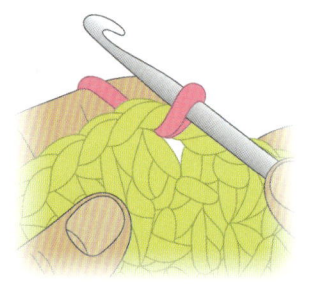

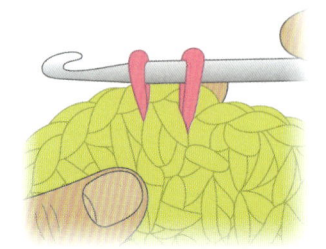

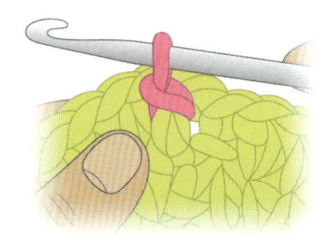

1 Using a contrast yarn, make a slip knot (see page 133). Holding the yarn with the slip knot behind the work and the hook in front, insert the hook between two stitches from front to the back and catch the slip knot behind the work with the hook. Draw the slip knot back through, so there is 1 loop on the hook at the front of the work.

2 Insert the hook between the next 2 stitches, yarn over hook and draw a loop through to the front. You will now have 2 loops on the hook.

3 Pull the first loop on the hook through the second loop to complete the first slip stitch on the surface of the work. Repeat steps 2 and 3 to make the next slip stitch. To join two ends with an invisible join, cut the yarn and thread onto a yarn needle. Insert the needle up through the last stitch, into the first stitch as if you were crocheting it, then into the back loop of the previous stitch. Fasten off on the wrong side.

Embroidery

These decorative hand-sewing techniques are used to add mouths, eyes and noses to some of the projects.

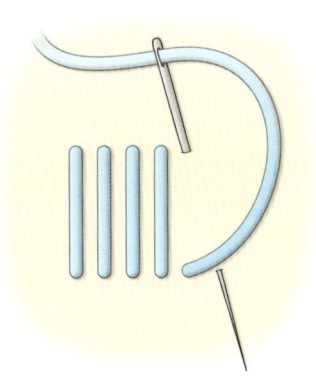

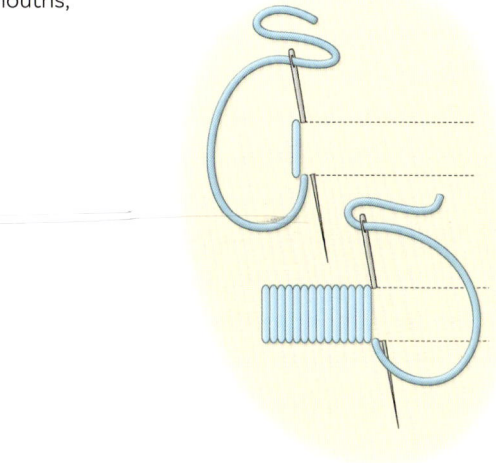

Straight stitch
Bring the needle through to the surface of the fabric and then take it back down to create a small straight stitch. These can be worked as part of a mouth design.

Satin stitch
Bring the needle up to the surface of the fabric, then take it back down at the selected point, drawing the yarn flush against the fabric. Bring the needle back up and down again next to the previous stitch. Continue in this manner, drawing the yarn smoothly against the surface of the fabric to fill the chosen area. The stitches should be close together, with no fabric visible in between them. They can be worked to create eyes or a nose on your finished crocheted cat project.

Adding safety eyes/noses
Note: If you're making a project for a young child or if it will be within reach of a young child, instead of adding a safety nose and eyes, embroider these features using straight stitch and satin stitch (see above).

Insert each eye from the front and make sure both eyes are completely level and sitting on the same round before you secure the safety catches at the back. The flat piece of the safety catch is pushed toward the crochet piece from the inside. Use the same method to insert the safety nose.

A safety eye insertion tool will make fitting the eyes easier. This usually consists of a piece of metal or plastic with holes for extra leverage when securing the eye washers.

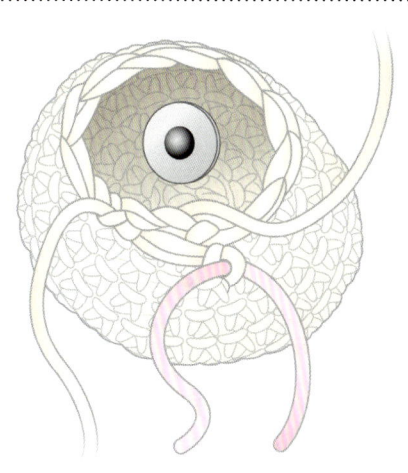

Adding fur
Adding the fur on the face can be done in two ways, either with a crochet hook or by threading each strand through with a yarn needle and then tying the ends into a knot close to the fabric. The needle is better for getting into small areas, such as around the eyes.

To add a piece of "fur" using a crochet hook, take two strands of yarn and fold them in half. Insert the crochet hook in the first stitch and hook the folded yarn loop. Pull the loop through about a third of the way. Now open up the loop (both pieces of yarn) and slip the ends of the yarn (all 4 ends) through the loop. Gently pull it tight to create the first piece of fur. Repeat to cover the project in fur as per the pattern instructions. You may need to adjust the ends as you tighten to get them all even.

Adding tassels and fringes
Tassels are single clusters of knotted yarn ends. Use the same method as for "adding fur" to add tassels along the edge of your project to create a fringe.

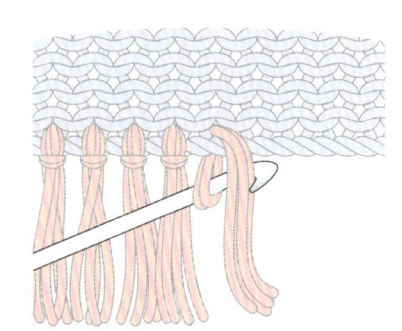

Adding whiskers

If desired, you can add whiskers to your finished cat project. You will need some medium-strength fishing line and craft glue.

Note: If you're giving the project to a young child, omit the whiskers or embroider them on in yarn with straight stitch (see page 141) instead.

Cut three lengths of fishing line, each approx. 7in (18cm). Push each piece of fishing line through the snout into position. The three pieces should be equal distances apart. Use the photograph in the project as a guide. Trim the whiskers to the length desired. Add a small dab of glue at each point where the whiskers enter the snout to hold them in place.

Abbreviations

Approx.	approximately
BP	work stitch around post of next stitch from back to front
BLO	work in the back loop only
ch	chain
cont	continue
dc	double crochet
FLO	work in the front loop only
FP	work stitch around post of next stitch from front to back
hdc	half double crochet
sc	single crochet
sc2tog	single crochet next two stitches together
sl st	slip stitch
st(s)	stitch(es)
[ ]	work stitches inside square brackets the number of times stated

Special abbreviations

FPdc (front post double crochet): a double crochet worked by inserting your hook around the post of the next stitch from front to back to front, rather than into the top two loops of a stitch as you normally would.

BPdc (back post double crochet): a double crochet worked by inserting your hook around the post of the next stitch from back to front to back, rather than into the top two loops of a stitch as you normally would.

Crochet stitch conversion chart

Crochet stitches are worked in the same way in both the UK and the USA, but the stitch names are not the same and identical names are used for different stitches. Below is a list of the UK terms used in this book, and the equivalent US terms.

US TERM	UK TERM
single crochet (sc)	double crochet (dc)
half double crochet (hdc)	half treble (htr)
double crochet (dc)	treble (tr)
triple treble (trtr)	double treble (dtr)
gauge	tension
yarn over hook (yoh)	yarn round hook (yrh)

Suppliers

We cannot cover all stockists here, so please explore the local yarn shops and online retailers in your own country. If you wish to substitute a different yarn for the one recommended in the pattern, try the Yarnsub website for suggestions: www.yarnsub.com.

King Cole yarns
www.kingcole.com

USA
LoveCrafts
Online sales
www.lovecrafts.com

Knitting Fever Inc.
www.knittingfever.com

WEBS
www.yarn.com

Michaels
Craft supplies
www.michaels.com

UK
LoveCrafts
Online sales
www.lovecrafts.com

Wool
Yarn, hooks
Store in Bath
+44 (0)1225 469144
www.woolbath.co.uk

Wool Warehouse
Online sales
www.woolwarehouse.co.uk

Laughing Hens
Online sales
Tel: +44 (0) 1829 740903
www.laughinghens.com

John Lewis
Yarns and craft supplies
Telephone numbers of stores on website
www.johnlewis.com

Hobbycraft
Yarns and craft supplies
www.hobbycraft.co.uk

Australia
Black Sheep Wool 'n' Wares
Retail store and online
Tel: +61 (0)2 6779 1196
www.blacksheepwool.com.au

Sun Spun
Retail store (Canterbury, Victoria) and online
Tel: +61 (0)3 9830 1609
www.sunspun.com.au

Acknowledgments

Thank you to the following people:

My husband Stuart and daughter Rebecca for all your help and support.

Joanne Whitehead at King Cole Yarns for all your help and advice with yarns for the patterns.

index